THE
TEX~MEX
SLOW COOKER

THE COUNTRYMAN PRESS
A division of W. W. Norton & Company
Independent Publishers Since 1923

THE TEX-MEX SLOW COOKER

100 DELICIOUS RECIPES FOR EASY EVERYDAY MEALS

VIANNEY RODRIGUEZ

This cookbook is dedicated to my daughter and sidekick in the kitchen, Angelica Maria. Thank you for always pushing me out of my comfort zone, for inspiring me to do more, and for bringing all of your heart and soul to *Sweet Life*. You put the boom-boom into my heart, and because of you, my little blog has grown into so much more than I ever thought it could be. Here's to many more years of spending time in the kitchen together cooking family dinners. Cooking with you has been one of the major highlights of my life and I'm glad we are able to create new family recipes together to pass on for future generations. I can't wait to see what amazing recipes you come up with on your own, my future chef.

CONTENTS

INTRODUCTION

Texas: We're famous for our gorgeous blue bonnets, our brisket, and our tall glasses of refreshing sweet tea. I'm a native South Texan (born and raised!), and I've spent the past six years perfecting some of my favorite Tex-Mex recipes. With *The Tex-Mex Slow Cooker*, I'm celebrating a childhood dream: writing my very first Tex-Mex cookbook. This book is a reflection of the flavors of my childhood, with my own special twist on the classics. By adapting these recipes for the slow cooker, I hope to help you spend less time in the kitchen and more time enjoying soul-satisfying meals with your family and friends.

SOUTH TEXAS FOOD CULTURE

Raised by Mexican parents, I was fortunate enough to benefit from Mexican traditions as well as the fusion food culture of Tejanos—tenderly known as Tex-Mex. With everything from brisket tacos to guava Champagne, Tex-Mex cuisine is a blend of two incredible food cultures I love.

South Texas is the birthplace of some of the most unique flavors in the world. If living here has taught me anything, it's that combining distinct flavors can make your food—and your life—way more exciting. A childhood spent near the Gulf Coast meant that I've always had access to amazing tacos, the freshest seafood you can imagine, and some pretty incredible beaches. And I wouldn't trade that for the world. South Texas is truly a magical place, and I feel blessed every day to call its Coastal Bend region my home.

My blog, SweetLifeBake.com, is a celebration of south Texas culture and my childhood memories of being raised in a kitchen filled with laughter, stories, love, and the wafting aroma of fresh tortillas on the *comal. Sweet Life*'s focus is a delicious blend of traditional Mexican, Tex-Mex, and Texan cuisines; it's where I share my passion for intense flavors, fresh ingredients, and the importance of creating food memories with the people you love. Every post on *Sweet Life* is filled with the vibrant culture of south Texas, so it's not just about our amazing food. Here in south Texas, we've also perfected some pretty incredible cocktail flavors as a result of our unique cultural fusion. In these pages, you'll find cocktails like my Ruby Red Paloma Punch (page 171) and Spiked Café de Olla (page 186) that will leave you wanting more.

So if you're ready to try some amazing recipes, let's dig in! Here, you'll find nearly one hundred recipes including everything from breakfast to appetizers to entrees to desserts—all you'll ever need to cook up the perfect south Texas meal. As a proud Tejana, I invite you to join me on this journey, and to experience all the rich culture Texas has to offer.

WHY YOU SHOULD BE SLOW COOKING

Here in south Texas, it's hot. Really hot. As we often say, it's 100 degrees in the shade. In conditions like that, we're not about to spend the day laboring over a hot stove or cranking up the oven. In the summer, South Texans do two things—we grill, and we load up our slow cookers with goodness.

One of the great things about slow cookers is that they don't use a lot of energy or give off much heat, so they keep the house cool and—most importantly—they allow you to relax and let great food cook itself. Why should you sweat it out, rushing back and forth in the kitchen? And when it comes to entertaining, well, forget it. If south Texas culture is about anything, it's about entertaining the people you love by sharing both great food and memorable stories. You need to be with your guests to share those stories, so slow cooking is a great way to get out of the kitchen and back with your guests.

Another of my favorite things about my slow cooker is that I can set it up in the morning and then come home after a long day to a home-cooked dinner. My life is busy, busy, busy. I never know what to expect each day, but I can always rely on my slow cooker to get the job done. Simply pile your ingredients high, set the timer, and let the appliance do the work for you—that's all it takes.

How to Choose a Slow Cooker

I still remember when I got my first slow cooker. I was a new mom and military wife looking for easy ways to get meals on the table. I knew a few things about slow cookers, but I soon discovered that there were plenty of things I didn't know. To help you get the most out of your slow cooker and make the best possible meals, I've put together a few tips to help you choose the right slow cooker for you.

HOW BIG SHOULD MY SLOW COOKER BE?

Size matters. When choosing your slow cooker, one of your first considerations should be its size. Think about how many people you're cooking for, what types of recipes you plan to cook, and whether or not you're a fan of leftovers. If you're cooking for a large family, or you wish to cook in large quantities for other reasons, it's best to go with a larger (at least 6-quart) slow cooker. If you're generally cooking for a smaller crowd, or plan to use it for making appetizers, sides, drinks, desserts, or small quantities of food, you might want to consider a smaller (3- to 4-quart) cooker. Following is a simple table that can help you decide what size slow cooker is best for you:

2 to 3 people = 3 to 5 quarts
4 to 5 people = 5 to 6 quarts
6+ people = 6+ quarts

SHOULD I GET A MANUAL OR AN AUTOMATIC SLOW COOKER?

There are two different kinds of slow cookers: the programmable kind, which you can set on a timer, and the manual kind, which you simply turn on to start cooking. Which is best for you depends a lot on your cooking style. If you're someone who likes to set and forget your slow cooker while you run errands or take care of other things, and if you don't want to worry about your food being overcooked, choose a slow cooker with a timer, as it'll allow you some peace of mind. These slow cookers automatically switch to the warm setting once the timer expires, instead of allowing your food to continue (over)cooking.

If you're usually home (or nearby), a manual slow cooker might work for you. They're usually less expensive and great for beginners or anyone who's got the time to keep watch as it cooks.

WHICH SLOW COOKER SHOULD I BUY?

Finding the right slow cooker for you might take some trial and error, but doing considerable research is the best way to make sure you pick the right cooker for your needs. Ask around. Talk to your family and friends to find out what slow cookers they use. Ask if they can recommend a certain brand, and what they find most useful about the slow cooker they chose. Also, don't forget to check online reviews of slow cookers before you buy; YouTube is a great place to look when researching slow cookers.

Slow-Cooking Tips and Tricks

Below are a few of my favorite tips and best practices for using a slow cooker.

- Every slow cooker is different. Cooking times and results may vary, so it's best to try out a few simple recipes to get a feel for how your slow cooker works. The first few times you use it, make some notes about how fast or slow your cooker makes each recipe. Some are faster (or slower) than others.

- Slow cookers work best when they're two-thirds to three-quarters full. Too little food can cause your recipe to overcook or burn, and too much might mean adding to the cooking time to make sure everything gets done. Make sure you adjust your cooking time based on how full your slow cooker is.

- Some recipes recommend a specific size of slow cooker. Follow the instructions as much as possible, and if you're not able to do so, adjust your cooking time accordingly, as the size and fullness of your slow cooker will affect the cooking time for your recipe.

- Large slow cookers can be used for everything from cooking hams and turkeys to making large batches of soups and stews. Because of their size, they making cooking for a crowd a snap and are great for holiday parties.

- Always remember to keep the lid on. The more often you lift the lid to check on the food, the more heat (and valuable cooking time!) is lost. You may have to add more cooking time if you check on the food frequently. If you do have to check the food, try to do so during the last 30 minutes of cooking, when the food is almost done.

- When possible, plan your meals ahead of time. If you have a busy day planned, prep your ingredients the night before, add them to the cooker in the morning, and set the cooking time (if your cooker has a timer) so it will reset to warm once the cooking is done. Doing so will save you a ton of time!

- If you have extra time, add extra flavor by browning your vegetables, meats, and other ingredients on the stovetop before adding them to your slow cooker. After you're done, deglaze all the delicious brown bits from the pan and pour that rich, golden liquid into your slow cooker—creating a dish packed with flavor.

NOTE: WHEN CREATING MOST OF THE RECIPES IN THIS BOOK, I USED A 6-QUART SLOW COOKER. WHEN I'VE USED A SMALLER ONE, I'VE NOTED THE RECOMMENDED SIZE.

Minimum Internal Temperatures

Watch your temperatures. Different foods have to be cooked to different temperatures in order to avoid foodborne illnesses. Following are the FDA's recommendations for minimum internal temperatures:

Beef, pork, veal, and lamb steaks/chops/roasts	145°F
Ground meats	160°F
Uncooked ham	165°F
Cooked ham (for reheating)	140°F
Poultry	165°F
Eggs	160°F
Fish and shellfish	145°F
Leftovers and casseroles	165°F

INGREDIENTS USED IN THIS BOOK

From cilantro and poblanos to plenty of lime juice, many of the ingredients used in this book are available in any supermarket. Tex-Mex cooking incorporates the flavors of Texas and Mexico, and Texans have embraced these flavors and woven them into their daily meals. Many supermarkets now carry a wide selection of Mexican cheeses, locally grown Texas produce, and chiles from Mexico. Even in my small town, I can find all that I need to make every dish in this cookbook. Specialty items such as *piloncillo*, *queso fresco*, *bolillos*, or *crema Mexicana* are available in most Latin markets. Substitutions can be made, but these ingredients are worth looking for as they add a depth of flavor that really makes the dish.

APPETIZERS

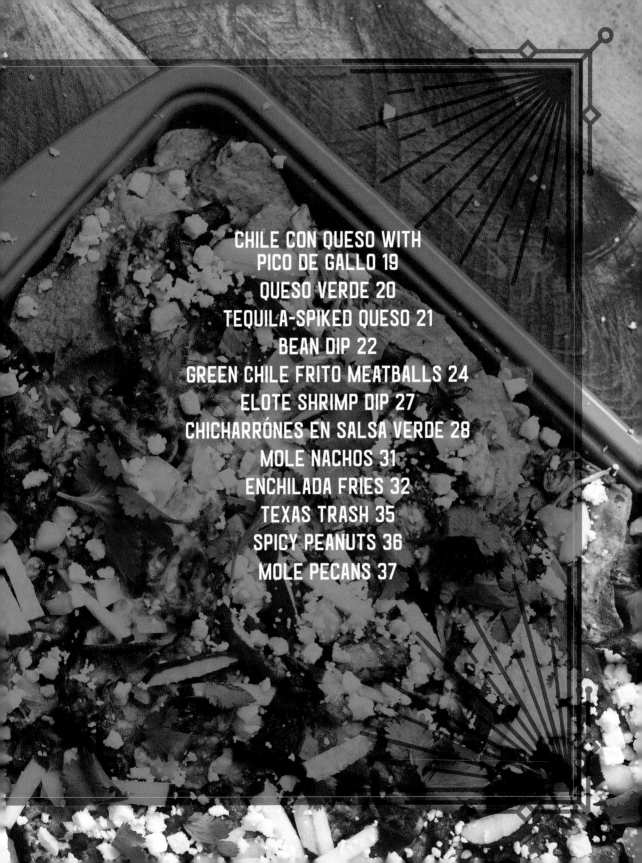

CHILE CON QUESO WITH
PICO DE GALLO 19
QUESO VERDE 20
TEQUILA-SPIKED QUESO 21
BEAN DIP 22
GREEN CHILE FRITO MEATBALLS 24
ELOTE SHRIMP DIP 27
CHICHARRÓNES EN SALSA VERDE 28
MOLE NACHOS 31
ENCHILADA FRIES 32
TEXAS TRASH 35
SPICY PEANUTS 36
MOLE PECANS 37

CHILE CON QUESO WITH PICO DE GALLO

My Tío Israel made this queso for my older sister's and my joint birthday party the year she turned 15 and I turned 13. We rented the local church hall, set up a few speakers, and invited the entire school. *Mi mami* set up a buffet table with sandwiches and punch, and *mi tío* brought this hearty, slightly spicy queso in a slow cooker. It was the hit of the party, and I've been making it ever since. It's the perfect easy dish for entertaining!

SERVES 6 TO 8

1 pound breakfast sausage

1 (10-ounce) can Rotel tomatoes, undrained

1 (2-pound) block Velveeta cheese, cubed

Pico de Gallo (page 99)

Tortilla chips, for serving

Brown the sausage in a large nonstick skillet over medium-high heat until fully cooked. Remove from the heat and drain.

Combine the cooked sausage, Rotel tomatoes, and Velveeta cheese in a slow cooker and stir until well combined. Cover and cook on low for up to 2 hours, stirring occasionally. It is ready to serve once all the cheese has melted.

Reduce the setting to warm and serve the queso topped with the Pico de Gallo and with a generous portion of the tortilla chips.

QUESO VERDE

Every fiesta needs a great queso, and this Queso Verde is a no-fuss, hands-free appetizer. I always stash a few cups of my Salsa Verde in the freezer so I can easily whip up this dish.

SERVES 6 TO 8

2 cups shredded Monterey Jack

1 (8-ounce) package cream cheese, diced

1 cup Salsa Verde (page 92), plus more for serving

½ cup whole milk

1 (4-ounce) can diced green chiles (optional)

Tortilla chips, for serving

Combine the cheeses, Salsa Verde, milk, and green chiles, if using, in a slow cooker and stir until well combined. Cover and cook on low for 2 hours, stirring occasionally.

Reduce the setting to warm and garnish with the remaining Salsa Verde and tortilla chips. Serve warm.

NOTE: FULLY COOKED GROUND BEEF, SLICED CARNE ASADA, OR FAJITAS CAN BE ADDED TO THE QUESO DURING THE FINAL 30 MINUTES OF COOKING.

TEQUILA-SPIKED QUESO

Tequila makes everything better, and here in Texas, we love our tequila. From margaritas to fajitas to queso—in south Texas, we spike everything with tequila!

SERVES 4 TO 6

8 ounces chorizo sausage

1 tablespoon olive oil

½ cup diced poblano pepper, seeds removed and discarded

¼ cup diced onion

⅓ cup tequila

2 cups shredded Monterey Jack

Salsa, chopped fresh cilantro, and diced tomatoes, for serving

Cook the chorizo in a nonstick skillet over medium-high heat, breaking up the sausage with a spoon, for 3 to 4 minutes, or until fully cooked. Remove from the heat. Place the cooked sausage on a plate lined with paper towels to fully drain.

Drain the fat from the skillet, add the oil to it, and warm it over medium-high heat. Add the poblano pepper and onion and sauté for 2 to 3 minutes, until the onion is light and translucent. Remove from the heat.

Return the pan to medium-high heat and carefully add the tequila. Reduce the heat to low and simmer for 2 minutes, or until the tequila evaporates. Remove from the heat.

Combine the chorizo and sautéed poblano pepper–onion mixture in a slow cooker. Add the cheese, cover, and cook, stirring occasionally, on low for 2 hours.

Reduce the setting to warm. Garnish with the salsa, cilantro, and tomatoes and serve warm.

BEAN DIP

This hearty bean dip, one of the easiest recipes in this book, yields the most amazing flavor. A few cans of beans and some spices come together to create a dip that tastes like it's been simmering away on the stove all day. Yum!

SERVES 20

1 teaspoon olive oil

½ onion, chopped

2 garlic cloves, minced

3 to 4 cups Frijoles de la Olla (page 104) or 2 (15-ounce) cans pinto beans, drained and rinsed

2 (15-ounce) cans red beans, drained and rinsed

2 (15-ounce) cans black beans, drained and rinsed

2 (15-ounce) cans kidney beans, drained and rinsed

2 (15-ounce) cans Mexican-style diced tomatoes, undrained

½ cup chopped fresh cilantro leaves, plus more for garnish

2 teaspoons ground cumin

2 teaspoons chili powder

1 teaspoon salt

1 teaspoon freshly ground black pepper

Shredded Cheddar, fresh avocado slices, and Mexican *crema* or sour cream, for garnish

Warm the oil in a skillet over medium-high heat. Add the onion and sauté for about 3 minutes, or until the onion is light and translucent. Add the garlic and cook, stirring often, for 2 minutes. Remove from the heat.

Combine the sautéed onion and garlic, the beans, the tomatoes, the ½ cup cilantro, the cumin, the chili powder, the salt, and the black pepper in a slow cooker and stir until well combined. Cover and cook on low for 2 hours.

Reduce the setting to warm. Stir and garnish with the remaining cilantro and the cheese, avocado, and *crema* or sour cream. Serve warm.

GREEN CHILE FRITO MEATBALLS

These meatballs pack a punch of Tex-Mex flavor! Vibrant green chiles and classic Frito corn chips make this an instant Texas favorite.

SERVES 8 TO 10 AS AN APPETIZER OR 4 TO 6 AS A MEAL

1 pound ground beef

1 pound pork breakfast sausage

1 cup Fritos corn chips, crushed

½ cup diced green chiles

½ cup finely diced onion

1 teaspoon ground cumin

1 teaspoon salt

1 teaspoon freshly ground black pepper

2 tablespoons olive oil

2 cups Salsa Verde (page 92)

Combine the beef, breakfast sausage, Fritos, green chiles, diced onion, cumin, salt, and black pepper in a large mixing bowl and mix the ingredients together with your hands until well blended. Shape the mixture into 1-inch balls.

Warm the oil in a skillet over medium-high heat. Add the meatballs and brown them in batches, cooking them for 3 minutes on each side. As the meatballs are browned, place them in a slow cooker. After all the meatballs have been browned, remove from the heat.

Pour the Salsa Verde over the meatballs. Cover and cook on low for 5 to 6 hours, or until the meatballs are fully cooked.

Reduce the setting to warm and serve. Allow to cool to room temperature before storing.

ELOTE SHRIMP DIP

This dish has all the flavor of *elote en vaso* (Mexican street corn in a cup), with a South Texan twist. With the addition of shrimp, chili powder, and fresh lime, this dip is the ultimate blend of Tex-Mex flavors.

SERVES 6 TO 8

1 (12-ounce) bag fully cooked small (51/60 count) shrimp

1 (15¼-ounce) can corn, drained

½ cup Mexican *crema*

¼ cup melted unsalted butter

1 cup Cojita cheese

2 teaspoons chili powder

Hot sauce (such as Valentina) and lime wedges, for serving

Liberally spray a slow-cooker liner with nonstick cooking spray.

Combine the shrimp, corn, *crema*, and butter in the slow cooker and stir until well combined. Cover and cook on low for 2 hours.

Reduce the setting to warm and sprinkle the cheese and chili powder over the dip. Serve warm with the hot sauce and lime wedges.

CHICHARRÓNES EN SALSA VERDE

There's nothing like a heaping pile of warm *chicharrónes* (fried pig skins) bathed in salsa verde and wrapped in a warm tortilla. You can also serve them over scrambled eggs. Use fresh *chicharrónes* from your local butcher for the best results.

SERVES 4 TO 6

1 pound *chicharrónes* (fried pig skins)

2 cups Salsa Verde (page 92)

Sliced radishes, warm tortillas, and salsa, for serving

Break the *chicharrónes* into bite-sized pieces and place the pieces in a slow cooker. Pour the Salsa Verde over the *chicharrónes*, cover, and cook on low for 1 hour. Stir.

Garnish with the radishes and serve warm with tortillas and salsa.

MOLE NACHOS

For family movie night, we whip up a baking sheet full of nachos and serve it family style. These nachos feature my favorite slow cooker Mole Sauce (page 98); it's rich, thick, and so addictive. You'll love it!

Serves 4 to 6

2 cups Shredded Chicken (page 52)

1 cup Mole Sauce (page 98)

4 cups tortilla chips

2 cups shredded Monterey Jack

1 cup crumbled *queso fresco*, ½ cup sliced radishes, and ⅓ cup chopped fresh cilantro leaves, for topping

Preheat the broiler.

Mix together the Shredded Chicken and the Mole Sauce in a large bowl.

Spread the tortilla chips evenly on a baking sheet and top them with the chicken mixture and the cheese. Broil for 8 to 10 minutes, or until the cheese is melted and the chicken is warmed through. Remove from the oven.

Top with the *queso fresco*, radishes, and cilantro and serve warm on the baking sheet.

ENCHILADA FRIES

This is my take on California's famous *carne asada* fries. Brimming with beef and enchilada sauce, these Tex-Mex fries are made to be shared and served with an icy cold beer.

Serves 4 to 6

1 (26-ounce) bag frozen French fries

2 cups shredded Beer-Braised Brisket (page 86) or Tomatillo Beef (page 44)

1 cup Red Enchilada Sauce (page 95)

2 cups shredded Cheddar

¼ cup diced onion and ¼ cup chopped fresh cilantro leaves, for topping

Sour cream, guacamole, and hot sauce or salsa, for serving

Prepare the French fries according to the package instructions.

Preheat the oven to 350°F.

Mix together the shredded brisket and the Red Enchilada Sauce in a large bowl.

Spread the fries evenly on a baking sheet and top them with the beef mixture and the cheese. Broil for 8 to 10 minutes, or until the cheese is melted and the beef is warmed through. Remove from the oven.

Top with the onion and cilantro. Serve warm on the baking sheet with the sour cream, guacamole, and hot sauce or salsa.

TEXAS TRASH

When the holidays roll around, you can find this Texas favorite at every potluck and party, or tucked away in tiny pouches alongside the Christmas gifts. We Texans can't get enough of our signature trail mix! I enjoy serving it warm at parties in my slow cooker. It's addictive!

SERVES 15 TO 20

3 cups Rice Chex cereal

3 cups Corn Chex cereal

3 cups Wheat Chex cereal

3 cups mixed nuts

2½ cups pretzels

¾ cup melted unsalted butter

1 teaspoon chili powder

1 teaspoon onion powder

1 teaspoon cayenne pepper

1 teaspoon ground cumin

1 teaspoon garlic powder

1 tablespoon Worcestershire sauce

1 tablespoon hot sauce (I recommend Valentina)

Combine the cereal, nuts, and pretzels in a slow cooker.

Whisk together the butter and spices in a large bowl until fully combined. Stir in the Worcestershire and hot sauces. Pour the contents of the bowl over the mixture in the slow cooker and stir until evenly coated.

Cover and cook on low for 3 hours, stirring once every hour to make sure the mixture cooks evenly. The edges of the cereal will begin to crisp after 2½ hours; continue stirring occasionally to allow all of the cereal mixture to crisp.

Reduce the setting to warm and serve warm. Provide your guests with small bowls so each can take a healthy share.

NOTE: BEFORE STORING ANY LEFTOVERS, ALLOW THE TEXAS TRASH TO COOL COMPLETELY. STORE IN A SEALED CONTAINER FOR UP TO 1 MONTH.

SPICY PEANUTS

Mi papi (my father) is addicted to two things: watching Pedro Infante movies and snacking on these spicy peanuts. This flavor-packed appetizer is a nod to my snack-loving *papi*.

MAKES 4 CUPS

6 tablespoons melted unsalted butter

¾ cup freshly grated *piloncillo* (see note)

3 tablespoons water, plus more as needed

1 tablespoon plus 1 teaspoon hot sauce, such as Valentina, plus more as needed

2 teaspoons Worcestershire sauce

1 teaspoon chili powder

1 teaspoon ground *chile de arbol*

4 cups peanuts, lightly salted

Place the butter in a large mixing bowl. Whisk in the *piloncillo*, 3 tablespoons of water, the hot sauce, Worcestershire sauce, chili powder, and *chile de arbol*. If the mixture is too thick, add more water, 1 teaspoon at a time, to thin the mixture. Taste and adjust the heat by adding more hot sauce if desired.

Place the peanuts in a slow cooker and pour the spice mixture over the peanuts. Stir until well combined. Cover and cook on low for 1½ hours, stirring occasionally.

Reduce the setting to warm and serve warm, or cool to room temperature and store in an airtight container. This recipe can easily be doubled.

NOTE: *PILONCILLO*, OR *PANELA*, IS AN UNREFINED MEXICAN SUGAR THAT CAN BE FOUND IN LATIN MARKETS. IT'S SOLD IN CONES, BLOCKS, OR ROUND DISCS; I SUGGEST USING A BOX GRATER TO GRATE *PILONCILLO*.

MOLE PECANS

Sugared pecans are a time-honored Christmas nibble you'll find in nearly every Texas home. Every family has its own secret recipe; we use a healthy dose of cinnamon in our version. Sometimes, I mix things up by serving these rich Mole Pecans instead of sugared pecans. If you can't find the dried chile powders called for in the recipe, feel free to grind up dried chiles in a coffee grinder and create your own.

MAKES 4 CUPS

6 tablespoons melted unsalted butter

¾ cup freshly grated *piloncillo* (see page 36)

3 tablespoons water, plus more as needed

2 tablespoons ancho chile powder

2 tablespoons guajillo chile powder

1 teaspoon ground cumin

1 teaspoon salt

½ teaspoon cayenne pepper

¼ teaspoon allspice

4 cups pecan halves

Place the butter in a large mixing bowl. Whisk in the *piloncillo*, 3 tablespoons of water, the ancho and guajillo chile powders, cumin, salt, cayenne, and allspice. If the mixture is too thick, add more water, 1 teaspoon at a time, to thin the mixture.

Place the pecans in a slow cooker and pour the spice mixture over the pecans. Stir until well combined. Cover and cook on low for 1½ hours, stirring occasionally.

Reduce the setting to warm and serve warm, or cool to room temperature and store in an airtight container. This recipe can easily be doubled.

MAIN COURSES

CARNE GUISADA

Carne guisada, which literally translates to "meat stew," is one of the most popular Tex-Mex dishes there is. This tender, slowly stewed meat is typically served with rice, refried beans, and plenty of warm tortillas. Browning the meat might seem like an extra step, but trust me, it's worth it. *Carne guisada* is magical!

SERVES 4 TO 6

4 pounds beef chuck roast,
  cut into 1-inch cubes
Salt and freshly ground black
  pepper to taste
2 tablespoons vegetable oil
2 cups chicken broth
1 (14-ounce) can diced tomatoes
1 medium white onion, diced
1 medium green bell pepper,
  seeded and diced
5 garlic cloves, minced
1 teaspoon chili powder
1 teaspoon ground cumin
1 teaspoon dried oregano
Warmed flour tortillas, prepared
  rice, and refried beans,
  for serving

Season the beef with the salt and black pepper. Warm 1 tablespoon of the oil in a large skillet over medium-high heat and brown the beef in batches, being careful not to overcrowd the skillet. As you brown the beef, add the additional tablespoon of oil if needed. Remove from the heat.

Combine the browned meat, chicken broth, tomatoes, onion, bell pepper, garlic, chili powder, cumin, and oregano in a slow cooker and stir until well combined. Cover and cook on low for 6 hours, or until the meat is fork tender.

Serve warm with the tortillas, rice, and refried beans.

COCHINITA PIBIL

Cochinita pibil hails from Mexico's Yucatán. The traditional method is to wrap a whole suckling pig in banana leaves and slow-roast it in a fire pit until tender. *Pibil* is Mayan for "buried," and a *cochinita* is a baby pig—hence the name. Citrus, a variety of spices, and achiote—a paste made from finely ground annatto seeds—give the dish its distinctive taste. By preparing this dish in my slow cooker, I can get the same moist, tender, earthy result without the fire pit and banana leaves. Sour oranges, which are traditionally used in this recipe, give this dish a depth of flavor, but they can be hard to find locally. I use a mix of orange, grapefruit, and lime juice in the marinade to try to replicate their unique flavor. Toasting the cinnamon sticks enhances their flavor. For optimal flavor, the pork should marinate overnight.

SERVES 6

6 tablespoons annatto seeds

1 tablespoon salt

2 teaspoons dried oregano

1 teaspoon freshly ground black pepper

½ teaspoon ground cumin

¼ teaspoon ground allspice

3 pounds boneless pork shoulder roast

2 (4-inch) cinnamon sticks

2 cups freshly squeezed grapefruit juice

2 cups freshly squeezed orange juice

½ cup freshly squeezed lime juice

4 garlic cloves, minced

1 bay leaf

Sliced radishes, crumbled *queso fresco* (optional), and warm corn tortillas or warm bread (if serving as *tortas*), for serving

Using a coffee grinder or a mortar and pestle, finely grind the annatto seeds.

Combine the ground annatto seeds with the salt, oregano, black pepper, cumin, and allspice in a small bowl. Rub the spice mixture all over the pork. Place the seasoned pork in a large, resealable plastic bag and refrigerate it overnight.

Toast the cinnamon sticks in a large skillet or *comal* over medium-high heat for 2 minutes on each side.

Combine the toasted cinnamon sticks, pork, citrus juices, garlic, and bay leaf in a slow cooker. Cover and cook on low for 6 to 8 hours, or until the meat is tender.

Transfer the pork to a serving platter and shred it. Drizzle the pork with the cooking juices. Serve warm garnished with the radishes and *queso fresco*, if using, and with the tortillas.

SLOW-COOKED TOMATILLO BEEF QUESADILLAS

I briefly worked at the San Antonio–based Tex-Mex chain Taco Cabana one summer when I was 18, manning the drive-through and assisting with food prep. I've never assembled so many quesadillas in my life—everyone wanted their beef quesadillas. This is my take on Taco Cabana's famous quesadillas; I make them when I crave a bit of that summer.

SERVES 6

3 pounds chuck roast, cut into
  2-inch dice

2 cups Salsa Verde (page 92)

2 cups chicken broth

2 medium tomatoes, diced

1 teaspoon ground cumin

1 teaspoon salt

1 teaspoon freshly ground black
  pepper

8 flour tortillas

2 cups shredded Monterey Jack

1 cup Pico de Gallo (page 99)
  and ½ cup sour cream, for
  topping

Combine the beef cubes, Salsa Verde, chicken broth, tomatoes, cumin, salt, and black pepper in a slow cooker and stir until well combined. Cover and cook on low for 6 to 8 hours, or until the meat is tender.

Preheat the broiler.

Warm the tortillas in a *comal* or dry skillet over medium-high heat. Remove from the heat and place the warmed tortillas on a baking sheet. Evenly divide the cheese among 4 of the tortillas, using tongs. Add the beef to each and then top each with the remaining 4 tortillas. Broil until the cheese melts. Remove from the oven.

Slice, top with the Pico de Gallo and sour cream, and serve warm.

NOTE: THIS RECIPE CAN ALSO BE SERVED AS A STEW OR LADLED INTO BOWLS OVER RICE. GARNISH WITH A DOLLOP OF SOUR CREAM AND A SPRINKLING OF CILANTRO.

CLASSIC MARGARITA FAJITAS

Nothing beats a classic. In this recipe, I've used all the flavors of a classic margarita to kick up fajitas. Tequila, orange juice, and plenty of lime juice create juicy, tender fajitas. Topped with avocado slices and a hefty sprinkle of salt, these fajitas are the perfect fiesta fare.

SERVES 6

3 pounds flank steak

1 cup tequila

1 cup freshly squeezed orange juice

Freshly squeezed juice of 3 limes

2 teaspoons salt, plus more for sprinkling

1 teaspoon freshly ground black pepper

2 onions, sliced

4 garlic cloves

Warm flour tortillas and fresh avocado slices, for serving

Place the flank steak in a slow cooker.

Whisk together the tequila, the orange and lime juices, the 2 teaspoons of the salt, and the black pepper in a small bowl. Pour the mixture over the steak; using tongs, turn the steak to ensure it is evenly coated. Top with the onion and garlic. Cover and cook on low for 6 to 8 hours, or until fork tender.

Slice the meat across the grain into strips. Sprinkle the slices with the salt and serve with the tortillas and avocado.

CHICKEN FAJITAS

Fajitas! Can't get enough of these Tex-Mex delights? Instead of waiting for your next visit to your favorite restaurant to enjoy them, why not try making them? Restaurant-quality fajitas are one of the easiest meals you can make at home—all you need is a few ingredients and a slow cooker.

These Chicken Fajitas, which cook up in no time, are a great go-to for a family get-together or party and are perfect served family style. Set up a taco bar, complete with different toppings—salsa, sliced onions, radishes, cheeses, and *crema* or sour cream. Your guests will have a great time customizing their tacos.

SERVES 6

4 pounds boneless, skinless
chicken breasts

1 teaspoon ground coriander

1 teaspoon ground cumin

1 teaspoon dried oregano

1 teaspoon salt

1 teaspoon freshly ground black
pepper

1 cup freshly squeezed orange
juice

1 red bell pepper, sliced, seeds
removed and discarded

1 yellow bell peppers, sliced,
seeds removed and discarded

1 poblano pepper, sliced, seeds
removed and discarded

Warm flour tortillas and choice
of toppings (see headnote), for
serving

Combine the chicken, coriander, cumin, oregano, salt, and black pepper in a slow cooker. Add the orange juice and, using tongs, turn the chicken to ensure it is evenly coated. Add the peppers, cover, and cook for 4 hours on high or 6 hours on low.

Slice the chicken into strips and serve warm with the tortillas and your choice of toppings.

CHICKEN TORTAS WITH TEQUILA-AVOCADO CREMA

A *torta* is a Mexican sandwich often eaten for lunch or on the go. Growing up, *mi mami* would pack us a few *tortas*, plus a thermos full of ice-cold *agua fresca,* to enjoy at the beach. On a sunny day, a big, messy *torta* really hits the spot.

A *torta* is typically made with a *bolillo. Bolillos* are fluffy, soft rolls with a crispy exterior—the perfect vessel for housing plenty of shredded chicken. I give these *tortas* a grown-up kick by drizzling them with my Tequila–Avocado Crema.

SERVES 4

For the Tequila–Avocado Crema:

2 avocados, skinned and pitted

¼ cup Mexican *crema*

½ cup chopped fresh cilantro leaves

Freshly squeezed juice of 1 lime

¼ cup tequila

½ teaspoon salt, plus more as needed

½ teaspoon freshly ground black pepper, plus more as needed

For the Tortas:

4 *bolillos*, halved

2 cups prepared Shredded Chicken (page 52) or store-bought rotisserie chicken, warmed

Tortilla chips, for serving

Make the Tequila–Avocado Crema:

Place all of the *crema* ingredients in a blender and blend until smooth. Taste and adjust the seasoning if needed.

Make the Tortas:

Warm the sliced *bolillos* in the oven. Top the 4 bottom halves of each *bolillo* with ½ cup of the Shredded Chicken. Drizzle the Tequila–Avocado Crema over each mound of Shredded Chicken. Top with the remaining 4 top halves of each *bolillo* and serve with the tortilla chips.

SHREDDED CHICKEN

Shredded chicken is an essential base ingredient for many of the recipes in this cookbook. This recipe is an easy way to make it at home and bypass those boring frozen or deli rotisserie chickens. Use this Shredded Chicken to make tostadas, tacos, flautas, or enchiladas. Try it in my Chicken Tortas with Tequila–Avocado Crema (page 51), Enchilada Casserole (page 75), Mole Tacos (page 81), and Pozole Verde con Pollo (page 64) recipes.

SERVINGS VARY BY RECIPE

4 pounds boneless skinless
   chicken breasts or thighs
2 teaspoons salt
1 teaspoon freshly ground black
   pepper
2 Roma tomatoes, coarsely sliced
1 onion, sliced
2 garlic cloves
1 bunch fresh cilantro, washed and
   tied together with kitchen twine
Water to cover

Place the chicken in a slow cooker and sprinkle it with the salt and black pepper. Add the tomatoes, onion, garlic, and cilantro. Add enough water to cover the chicken, cover, and cook on low for 6 hours, or until the chicken is tender.

Shred the chicken with forks. Use in your choice of recipes or freeze for later use.

NOTE: THIS RECIPE IS GREAT FOR TACOS. SERVE THE SHREDDED CHICKEN WARM WITH WARMED FLOUR TORTILLAS, AND TOP EACH WITH DICED TOMATOES AND RED ONION.

GUAVA DRUMSTICKS

Drumsticks are one of those go-to, no-fail recipes that make dinnertime easy. I ate a lot of baked chicken growing up, especially after *mi mami* began working two jobs. She relied on quick and easy recipes that she knew could feed us all and required little to no effort. These guava drumsticks are comforting and kid-friendly—perfect when you need to feed a crowd.

SERVES 6

12 bone-in skin-on chicken legs

4 cups guava juice

Freshly squeezed juice of 1 lemon

¼ cup olive oil

4 garlic cloves, minced

2 tablespoons agave syrup

2 teaspoons ground cumin

1 teaspoon onion powder

1 teaspoon salt

1 teaspoon freshly ground black
   pepper

Liberally spray a slow-cooker liner with nonstick cooking spray and place the chicken in the slow cooker.

Whisk together the guava and lemon juices, oil, garlic, agave syrup, cumin, onion powder, salt, and black pepper in a small bowl and pour the mixture over the chicken. Cover and cook on low for 4 hours.

Serve warm.

MIGAS CASSEROLE

Migas are a breakfast favorite in every corner of Texas. I've taken the classic skillet *migas* and transformed them into a low-and-slow, cheesy *migas* casserole. Put on a pot of coffee, invite a few friends over, and enjoy this *migas* casserole for brunch.

SERVES 4

4 cups homemade tortilla chips from about 12 corn tortillas (see note) or high-quality store-bought tortilla chips
8 large eggs, lightly whisked
¼ cup whole milk
1 (10-ounce) can Mexican-style diced tomatoes
2 cups shredded Cheddar
Salt and freshly ground black pepper to taste
Salsa, sour cream, and fresh diced avocado, for topping
Warm tortillas, for serving (optional)

Place the tortilla chips in the slow cooker.

Whisk together the eggs, milk, tomatoes, and cheese in a medium bowl and season with the salt and black pepper. Pour the egg mixture over the tortilla chips and stir until the chips are evenly coated. Cover and cook on low for 4 hours, or until all of the egg mixture is firm.

Serve warm topped with the salsa, sour cream, and avocado. If you wish to serve the casserole as tacos, serve with the tortillas as well.

NOTE: TO MAKE HOMEMADE TORTILLA CHIPS, WARM 1 INCH OF VEGETABLE OIL IN A DEEP SKILLET OVER MEDIUM-HIGH HEAT. SLICE THE CORN TORTILLAS INTO FOURTHS AND FRY THEM UNTIL THEY ARE LIGHTLY CRISP. REMOVE TO A PLATE LINED WITH PAPER TOWELS AND SEASON WITH SALT. USE THESE CHIPS TO MAKE *MIGAS* OR *CHILAQUILES*, OR ENJOY THEM WITH SALSA AND QUESO.

SHRIMP PICO

I had a version of this dish at a restaurant in Rockport, a town on the Texas coast. I vividly remember the plump Texas shrimp sautéed with all the wonderful flavors of *pico de gallo*. Here's my slow-cooker take on the dish.

SERVES 4

1 pound shrimp, peeled and deveined

1 (10-ounce) can Mexican-style diced tomatoes, undrained

1 cup chicken broth

1 onion, diced

1 cup chopped fresh cilantro leaves, plus more for serving

1 jalapeño pepper, minced (optional)

1½ teaspoons salt

1 teaspoon freshly ground black pepper

Freshly squeezed juice of 1 lime

Cooked white rice, for serving

Combine the shrimp, the tomatoes, the chicken broth, the onion, 1 cup of the cilantro, the jalapeño (if using), the salt, and the black pepper in a slow cooker and stir until well combined. Cover and cook on low for 2½ hours.

Stir in the lime juice, garnish with the remaining cilantro, and serve warm with the rice.

CHICKEN VERDE

This is an easy, filling weeknight dinner that everyone will love. My Chicken Verde comes together quickly and is ready when you get home from work. Served warm, with a side of beans and rice, this recipe has a permanent spot on my weekly meal planning menu. You can also use Chicken Verde to make puffy tacos, chicken burritos, chicken tostadas, or chicken enchiladas.

SERVES 6 TO 8

2½ pounds bone-in chicken thighs (about 8)
Salt and freshly ground black pepper to taste
4 cups Salsa Verde (page 92)
1 teaspoon garlic powder
1 teaspoon ground cumin

Season the chicken with the salt and black pepper and place it in a slow cooker. Add the Salsa Verde, garlic powder, and cumin and, using tongs, turn the chicken thighs to ensure they are evenly coated. Cover and cook on low for 8 hours or on high for 4 hours.

Using two forks, shred the chicken and remove and discard the bones.

NOTE: FOR TACOS, SERVE THE CHICKEN IN WARMED TORTILLAS WITH SLICED RADISHES, *QUESO FRESCO*, AND SALSA.

CALDO DE POLLO

Nothing beats the winter blues like a steamy bowl of *caldo de pollo*: it soothes the soul and warms the belly. This is my slow-cooker version of *mi mami's* famous *caldo de pollo*.

SERVES 8

1 whole fryer chicken, cut into 8 pieces

1 onion, sliced in half and skin removed

2 garlic cloves, minced

4 large carrots, cut into 1-inch pieces

4 celery stalks, cut into 1-inch pieces

2 teaspoons salt

1 teaspoon freshly ground black pepper

1 teaspoon ground cumin

1 bay leaf

Water to cover

4 large russet potatoes, quartered

½ head cabbage, quartered

Cooked white rice, warm corn tortillas, and lime wedges, for serving

Combine the chicken, onion, garlic, carrots, celery, salt, black pepper, cumin, and bay leaf in a slow cooker. Cover with water, cover, and cook on low for 4 hours.

After 4 hours, add the potatoes and cabbage. Cover and cook for 1 hour, or until the potatoes are fork tender.

Serve warm with the rice, corn tortillas, and lime wedges.

POZOLE VERDE CON POLLO

Bring on the steaming bowls of *pozole*! When I was growing up, my mom would start a big pot of *pozole* in the morning and let it simmer away all day on the stove, filling our home with warm, comforting aromas. After we finished playing board games or doing our homework, she'd ready the table and set out small bowls brimming with various garnishes to add to our *pozole*—fresh ingredients like radishes, cilantro, Pico de Gallo (page 99), avocado, or *queso fresco*.

My dad would ladle bowl after bowl of rich *pozole*, making sure each of us had plenty of the hominy (our favorite) in our bowls. Our bellies welcomed spoon after spoon of this comforting soup. The warmth of the kitchen, and the memory of being surrounded by *familia*, makes this soup dear to my heart.

Pozole (which translates to "hominy") is a traditional Mexican soup that can be made with chicken or pork. Variations include *pozole rojo* (red *pozole*, made with chiles) or *pozole verde* (green *pozole*, made with tomatillos). I love my mom's original *pozole rojo* recipe, but on days I need an extra dose of comfort, or if I'm missing my family, I make this easy *pozole verde con pollo*. I also take this opportunity to give my mom's traditional recipe a few tweaks, incorporate my favorite spices, and adapt the recipe with a few shortcuts—giving this dish a new, unexpected spin.

SERVES 6 TO 8

1 (28-ounce) can tomatillos, drained

2 (14-ounce) cans chicken broth

1 medium onion, chopped

1 cup coarsely chopped fresh cilantro leaves, plus more for garnish

2 garlic cloves

2 teaspoons salt

1 teaspoon freshly ground black pepper

1 teaspoon ground cumin

1 teaspoon dried oregano

4 cups prepared Shredded Chicken (page 52) or store-bought rotisserie chicken

2 (15-ounce) cans hominy, rinsed and drained

Fresh avocado slices, sliced radishes, and lime wedges, for garnish

Combine the tomatillos, 1 cup of the chicken broth, the onion, 1 cup of the cilantro, the garlic, the salt, the black pepper, the cumin, and the oregano in a blender and blend until smooth.

Combine the tomatillo mixture, the remaining chicken broth, the Shredded Chicken, and the hominy in a slow cooker. Cover and cook on low for 4 hours.

Ladle the *pozole* into bowls. Garnish with the remaining cilantro, the avocado slices, the radishes, and the lime wedges and serve.

TAMARIND CHIPOTLE PORK TOSTADAS

This recipe will kick up your weeknights by adding a hint of spice to the mix. Chipotle peppers and tamarind soda transform an ordinary standby pork shoulder into a fiesta for your mouth.

SERVES 6

For the Chipotle Pork:

2 teaspoons chili powder

2 teaspoons salt

1 teaspoon ground cumin

1 teaspoon dried oregano

1 teaspoon freshly ground black pepper

4 pounds bone-in pork shoulder

1 (15-ounce) can diced tomatoes

1 (12-ounce) bottle tamarind soda (I recommend Jarritos)

1 onion, sliced

5 garlic cloves

3 chipotle peppers in adobo sauce, chopped

For the Pickled Red Onions:

1 cup water

½ cup granulated sugar

¼ cup rice vinegar

2 red onions, thinly sliced

2 tablespoons freshly squeezed lime juice

Make the Chipotle Pork:

Combine the chili powder, salt, cumin, oregano, and black pepper in a small bowl. Rub the spice mix over the pork shoulder and place it in a slow cooker.

Add the tomatoes, tamarind soda, onion, garlic, and chipotles to the slow cooker. Cover and cook for 8 hours on low.

Shred the pork shoulder using two forks; remove and discard the bone. Set aside.

Make the Pickled Red Onions:

Combine the water, sugar, and rice vinegar in a saucepan over medium-high heat and bring to a boil. Cook, stirring constantly, until the sugar dissolves. Remove from the heat. Add the onions and set aside to cool completely.

Add the lime juice and stir until well combined.

continued

For the Tostadas:

12 tostada shells

2 cups refried black beans, warmed

Diced fresh avocado and lime wedges, for garnish

Make the Tostadas:

Spread each tostada shell with equal portions of the black beans. Top with the shredded pork and garnish with the avocado and lime wedges. Serve with the Pickled Red Onions.

NOTE: PICKLED ONIONS CAN BE STORED IN AN AIRTIGHT CONTAINER FOR UP TO 2 WEEKS IN THE REFRIGERATOR. THEY'RE GREAT WITH TACOS, ENCHILADAS, OR NACHOS.

FRITO PIE

Simply put, a Frito Pie is a pile of Frito corn chips topped with chili, plenty of cheese, and diced onions. This Texas favorite is served at baseball games, movie theaters, and festivals. I like to serve mine in single-serving bags of Fritos to give my guests the full experience.

SERVES 10

2 teaspoons vegetable oil

2 pounds ground beef

1 (14-ounce) can tomato sauce

3 tablespoons chili powder

2 teaspoons garlic powder

1 teaspoon ground cumin

1 teaspoon salt

1 teaspoon freshly ground black pepper

10 (1-ounce) bags Fritos corn chips

2 cups shredded Cheddar

1 cup finely diced onion

Warm the oil in a large skillet over medium-high heat. Add the ground beef and cook, taking care to break up the meat with the back of spoon and stirring frequently, until it is fully browned and cooked through. Remove from the heat.

Stir in the tomato sauce, chili powder, garlic powder, cumin, salt, and black pepper. Pour the mixture into a slow cooker, cover, and cook on low for 6 hours.

Reduce the setting to warm.

To serve, cut open the tops of each bag of Fritos. Spoon the chili con carne over the Fritos, top each with the cheese and onions, and serve. (This dish can also be served in bowls.)

CHICKEN VERDE WITH NOPALES

A hearty, crowd-pleasing dish, my Chicken Verde with Nopales is a snap to pull together. It's perfect for entertaining—especially when I want to introduce my guests to the all the wonders of *nopales*, the paddles of the cactus plant. You can find them in Mexican markets, sold diced or in strips. Their taste is hearty, somewhat like a green bean. I like to serve this dish over rice to soak up all the tasty broth.

SERVES 6

6 skinless bone-in chicken breasts

1 (30-ounce) jar *nopales*, drained and rinsed

2 cups Salsa Verde (page 92)

1 cup chicken broth

1 teaspoon dried oregano

1 teaspoon salt

1 teaspoon freshly ground black pepper

1 cup Mexican *crema*

1 cup finely diced red onions and lime wedges, for garnish

Cooked white rice, for serving

Combine the chicken breasts, *nopales*, Salsa Verde, chicken broth, oregano, salt, and black pepper in a slow cooker. Using tongs, ensure that each piece of chicken is evenly coated. Cover and cook on low for 6 hours.

Stir in the *crema*, garnish with the red onions and lime wedges, and serve warm over the rice.

CHILAQUILES CASSEROLE

I am obsessed with *chilaquiles*; they are my ultimate brunch treat. Made with freshly fried tortillas swimming in sauce, shredded chicken, and plenty of cheese, this casserole is hands-down amazing. I enjoy making this for Sunday brunch, or for lunches when I need to use up some leftover homemade tortilla chips from a family gathering. I can easily put everything into the slow cooker, walk away, and enjoy my morning coffee—and cleanup is a breeze. Once my guests arrive, all I have to do is slice up some avocados.

SERVES 6

1½ cups Red Enchilada Sauce (page 95) or Enchilada Verde Sauce (page 96)

1 cup chicken broth

4 cups homemade tortilla chips (page 56) or high-quality store-bought tortilla chips

3 cups Shredded Chicken (page 52) or store-bought rotisserie chicken

2 cups shredded Monterey Jack Mexican *crema*, fresh avocado slices, and chopped fresh cilantro, for garnish

Liberally spray a slow-cooker liner with nonstick cooking spray.

Mix together the Red Enchilada Sauce and the broth in a large mixing bowl.

Combine the tortilla chips, Shredded Chicken, cheese, and the sauce-broth mixture in a slow cooker. Stir gently until the mixture is combined and all of the chips are coated with the sauce. Cover and cook on low for 4 hours, or until all the liquid is absorbed.

Serve warm garnished with the *crema*, avocado slices, and cilantro.

ENCHILADA CASSEROLE

Mi mami started making enchilada casseroles as her *familia* grew and grew, and she tired of hand-rolling all those enchiladas individually. I can't say I blame her—we're a big crowd. This enchilada casserole can be made with either green or red enchilada sauce, and feel free to swap out the Shredded Chicken for my Slow-Cooked Tomatillo Beef (page 44) or Chipotle Pork (page 67).

SERVES 6 TO 8

¼ cup vegetable oil, for frying

15 to 20 (6-inch) corn tortillas

2 cups Red Enchilada or Enchilada Verde Sauce (page 95 or 96)

4 cups Shredded Chicken (page 52) or store-bought rotisserie chicken

2½ cups shredded Monterey Jack

1 cup diced onion

Warm the vegetable oil in a nonstick skillet over medium-high heat. In batches, lightly fry each tortilla on both sides for about 1 minute each side; they should still be pliable when done. Transfer each from the pan to a paper towel–lined plate to drain. Continue until all the tortillas have been fried and then remove from the heat.

Liberally spray a slow-cooker liner with cooking spray. Place a fourth of the tortillas in a layer on the bottom of the slow cooker and then cover it with a fourth of the sauce. Add a fourth of the Shredded Chicken and sprinkle a fourth of the cheese and the onions over the chicken. Repeat until all of the ingredients have been used. Cover and cook on low for 4 hours, or until all of the liquid has been absorbed.

Serve warm.

TACOS DE LENGUA

Plenty of people are initially turned off by the idea of *lengua* (beef tongue), but little do they know—*lengua* is one of the tastiest dishes you can ask for. *Tacos de lengua*, a beloved south Texas treat, can be found on the menus of practically every restaurant from San Antonio to Brownsville.

SERVES 4

1 (3- to 4-pound) beef tongue

1 onion, skin removed and halved

5 garlic cloves

2 teaspoons salt

1 teaspoon freshly ground black
    pepper

1 bay leaf

Warm flour tortillas, diced
    radishes, chopped fresh cilantro,
    and lime wedges, for serving

Thoroughly rinse the beef tongue and place it in a slow cooker with the onion, garlic, salt, black pepper, and bay leaf. Cover and cook on low for 8 hours, or until the meat is tender when pierced with a knife.

Carefully remove the meat from the slow cooker. With a paring knife, remove and discard the skin and cut the meat into small dice.

Return the meat to the slow cooker and reduce the setting to warm. Serve warm with the tortillas, radishes, cilantro, and lime wedges.

TAMALE PIE

In the 19th century, Texans were introduced to tamales, and it was love at first bite! Making tamales at home can be time-consuming, so to cut down on time, home cooks created the Tamale Pie. Easy to prepare and loaded with flavor, this recipe will satisfy even your hungriest Texan!

SERVES 6 TO 8

For the Filling:

2 teaspoons oil

2 pounds ground beef

1 onion, diced

1 bell pepper, seeds removed and diced

1 teaspoon ground cumin

1 teaspoon salt

1 teaspoon freshly ground black pepper

2 cups frozen corn kernels

1 (14-ounce) can diced tomatoes

1½ cups Red Enchilada Sauce (page 95)

1 cup shredded Cheddar

For the Topping:

1 cup whole milk

2 large eggs

½ cup cornmeal

½ cup masa harina

½ teaspoon baking powder

1 cup shredded Cheddar

1 cup sour cream, for serving

Make the Filling:

Warm the oil in a large skillet over medium-high heat. Add the ground beef, onion, bell pepper, cumin, salt, and black pepper and cook, taking care to break up the beef with the back of a spoon and stirring frequently, until it is fully browned and cooked through. Remove from the heat and drain off any excess fat. Stir in the tomatoes, corn, Red Enchilada Sauce, and cheese until well combined.

Taste for seasoning, adjust if necessary, and spoon the filling into a slow cooker. Cover and cook on low for 6 hours.

Make the Topping:

Whisk together the milk and eggs in a medium bowl. While whisking constantly, add the cornmeal, masa harina, and baking powder. Continue whisking until fully combined and then stir in the cheese.

Spoon the topping evenly over the beef mixture and smooth it down with the back of spoon. Cover and cook on low for 1 hour, or until a toothpick inserted into the center comes out clean.

Serve warm with the sour cream.

CHILE RELLENO CASSEROLE

This dish has all the flavors of a chile relleno—without the extra steps. There's no need to stuff, bread, and individually fry each chile when you make this dish casserole style. Cook this casserole on low overnight to serve for breakfast, or crank it up to high to serve it for dinner. Whether I serve my chile relleno casserole for breakfast or dinner, it is always a hit at my table.

SERVES 8

8 poblano peppers
1 teaspoon vegetable oil
1 pound ground beef
½ cup diced onion
1 garlic clove, minced
12 large eggs
½ cup whole milk
1 teaspoon salt
1 teaspoon freshly ground black
  pepper
1½ cups shredded Monterey Jack,
  plus more for topping
Warm flour tortillas, for serving
  (optional)

Preheat the broiler and place the poblanos on a baking sheet.

Broil the poblanos for 4 to 6 minutes on each side, or until they are charred on all sides. Remove from the oven, cover with a dish towel, and set aside to steam for 10 minutes.

Remove and discard the poblanos' charred skin, stems, and seeds and slice the peppers into strips. Set aside.

Warm the oil in a nonstick pan over medium-high heat. Add the ground beef, onion, and garlic and cook for 8 to 10 minutes, or until fully browned and cooked through. Drain.

Liberally spray a slow-cooker liner with nonstick cooking spray. Add the ground beef mixture and the poblano strips.

Whisk together the eggs, milk, salt, and black pepper in a large bowl and pour the mixture over the beef and poblanos. Add 1½ cups of the cheese and stir until well combined. Cover and cook on low for 8 hours or on high for 4 hours.

Top with the remaining cheese and serve warm, or if serving as tacos, serve warm with the flour tortillas.

MOLE TACOS

Looking to feed a crowd? My Mole Tacos are the ultimate crowd pleaser. All you have to do is set up your slow cooker, and your guests are free to make their own tacos. Mole Tacos and ice-cold beers—it's a win-win.

SERVES 8

4 cups Shredded Chicken (page 52) or store-bought rotisserie chicken
2 cups Mole Sauce (page 98)
½ cup sesame seeds, for garnish
16 corn tortillas, warmed, for serving
Picked Red Onions (page 67), avocado, or salsa of choice, for serving (optional)

Combine the Shredded Chicken and Mole Sauce in a slow cooker. Cover and cook on low for at least 2 hours.

When ready to serve, reduce the setting to warm. Garnish with the sesame seeds and serve warm with the tortillas. These tacos can be served with Pickled Red Onions, avocado, or salsa of choice.

ANCHO CHILE CARNITAS

Weekends scream for piles and piles of juicy *carnitas*. From tacos to nachos to enchiladas, this shredded pork is super versatile. I use Mexican Coke and ancho chiles to give these *carnitas* a punch of flavor.

SERVES 10 TO 12

4 ancho chiles, stems and seeds removed

Water to cover

5 pounds boneless pork shoulder

1 (12-ounce) bottle Mexican Coke

1 onion, sliced

4 garlic cloves

Freshly squeezed juice of 1 lime

1 tablespoon ground cumin

1 tablespoon salt

2 teaspoons dried oregano

1 teaspoon freshly ground black pepper

1 bay leaf

1 bunch fresh cilantro, washed and tied together with kitchen twine

Warm corn tortillas, crumbled *queso fresco*, and sliced radishes, for serving

Place the chiles in a microwave-safe bowl and cover them with water. Microwave on high for 4 minutes. Remove from the microwave, cover, and set aside to steep for at least 10 minutes.

Cut the pork into large pieces and place them in a slow cooker. Add the chiles, Coke, onion, garlic, lime juice, cumin, salt, oregano, black pepper, and bay leaf and stir to ensure the pork is evenly coated. Place the cilantro over the pork, cover, and cook on low for 8 hours, or until the pork is fork tender.

Using two forks, shred the pork. Serve warm with the tortillas, *queso fresco*, and radishes as tacos, or use to make enchiladas, tostadas, or nachos.

PICADILLO

Comfort in a bowl: Picadillo is one of the easiest recipes in this cookbook. But don't be fooled by its ease—this beef soup is one of my most-requested recipes for Sunday family dinner. *Picadillo* gets its name from the word *picar,* which translates to "chopped."

SERVES 6

1 teaspoon vegetable oil

2 pounds ground beef

1 onion, diced

3 medium russet potatoes, peeled and diced into ½ inch cubes

1 green bell pepper, diced

1½ cups water

2 garlic cloves, minced

2 teaspoons salt

1 teaspoon freshly ground black pepper

Warm the oil in a skillet over medium-high heat. Add the ground beef and onion and cook, taking care to break up the beef with the back of a spoon, until it is fully cooked.

Combine the cooked ground beef–onion mixture, potatoes, bell pepper, water, garlic, salt, and black pepper in a slow cooker. Cover and cook on low for 8 hours, or until potatoes are tender.

Serve warm.

BEER-BRAISED BRISKET

Everyone loves brisket, a Texas staple. Texans—Tejanos—are obsessed. My Beer-Braised Brisket is fork tender, perfect for a crowd, and requires no babysitting. Place it in the slow cooker and go about your day. Your family will love it, and football fans will adore it!

SERVES 8 TO 10

1 onion, sliced

5 pounds beef brisket

1 (15-ounce) can diced tomatoes

1 (12-ounce) can Modelo beer

3 garlic cloves

1 tablespoon plus 1 teaspoon
  dried oregano

1 tablespoon salt

1 tablespoon freshly ground black
  pepper

Warm flour tortillas, cooked
  beans, and fresh avocado slices,
  for serving

Place the onion slices in a slow cooker and add the brisket, fat side up. Add the tomatoes, beer, garlic, oregano, salt, and black pepper. Cover and cook on low for 8 hours, or until the brisket is fork tender.

Carefully remove the brisket from the slow cooker. Slice or shred the brisket and return it to the slow cooker. Reduce the setting to warm. Serve warm with the tortillas, beans, and avocado slices.

SALSAS
AND SIDES

SALSA ROJA

My brother-in-law, Ruben, is addicted to salsa *picante*. You can always find a jar next to his plate at every meal. My version, an adaptation of the famous Pace Picante Sauce, which hails from Texas, is dedicated to him. Love ya, Ruben.

MAKES 4 CUPS

2 pounds fresh Roma tomatoes, halved

1 (28-ounce) can whole plum tomatoes

2 onions, skins removed and quartered

½ cup sliced pickled jalapeño peppers

1 teaspoon minced dried garlic or 2 cloves fresh garlic, minced

1 bunch fresh cilantro leaves, washed

Salt and freshly ground black pepper to taste

Combine the Roma tomatoes, canned tomatoes, onions, jalapeños, and dried garlic in a slow cooker. Cover and cook on low for 5 hours, or until the onions have softened.

Carefully add the mixture, along with the cilantro, to the bowl of a food processor fitted with the "S" blade. Pulse until the tomatoes are broken up, but the mixture is not pureed (the salsa should be chunky). Season with the salt and black pepper.

To serve the salsa at a party, return it to the slow cooker and reduce the setting to warm. You can also serve it warm or cold with tortilla chips. If serving cold, set aside to cool completely, and then store it in a sealed container in the refrigerator for up to 4 days. This salsa can also be frozen for up to 1 month and thawed for later use in small batches.

SALSA VERDE

From family meals to impromptu fiestas, I always make sure I have plenty of salsa on hand for my guests to enjoy. I make an extra-large batch on Sundays while I prep meals for the week. Putting all the ingredients in my slow cooker means less time spent over the stove and more time to focus on my family.

MAKES 6 TO 8 CUPS

4 pounds tomatillos, husks removed

3 jalapeño peppers

2 onions, peeled and halved

3 garlic cloves

1 cup water

1½ tablespoons salt, plus more to taste

2 teaspoons freshly ground black pepper, plus more to taste

2 teaspoons ground cumin

Preheat the broiler and place the tomatillos, jalapeños, onion, and garlic on a baking sheet.

Broil the vegetables and aromatics for 5 to 7 minutes, or until lightly charred. Remove from the oven.

Combine all of the ingredients in a slow cooker. Cover and cook for 2 hours on high or 4 hours on low.

Carefully blend the cooked Salsa Verde with an immersion blender or in batches using a blender until smooth. Season with additional salt and black pepper to taste, if desired, and serve.

RED ENCHILADA SAUCE

Whenever I visit a new Tex-Mex joint, I always order the cheese enchiladas. I am addicted to dark-hued red enchilada sauce. Instead of the usual chili powder, I opt to use dried chiles when making this rich and savory enchilada sauce. I also use tomatoes, which is not traditional, but when I was growing up, my *mami* grew the very best tomatoes—so it was only natural that they would find their way into my enchilada sauce.

MAKES 6 CUPS

6 ancho chiles

5 pasilla chiles

1 onion, sliced in half

3 tomatoes

4 garlic cloves

2 teaspoons salt, plus more to taste

1 teaspoon freshly ground black pepper, plus more to taste

1 teaspoon dried oregano

1 teaspoon ground cumin

1 tablespoon olive oil

NOTE: ENCHILADA SAUCE BECOMES THICKER AS IT COOLS; USE WATER OR CHICKEN BROTH TO THIN IT TO THE DESIRED CONSISTENCY.

Toast the ancho and pasilla chiles on a preheated *comal* or dry skillet for 10 to 15 seconds on each side. The chiles will puff up slightly and become toasted and pliable. Remove the chiles and set them aside to cool.

Return the same *comal* or skillet to the heat and sear the onion, tomatoes, and garlic for about 5 to 8 minutes, turning frequently, until the tomatoes' skins are lightly charred.

Remove and discard the chiles' stems and seeds. Combine the toasted chiles, the onion, tomatoes, garlic, 2 teaspoons of salt, 1 teaspoon of black pepper, the oregano, and the cumin in a slow cooker and cover the ingredients with water. Cover and cook on low for 6 hours.

Carefully blend the cooked sauce with an immersion blender or in batches using a blender until smooth. Add additional water if necessary, ½ cup at a time, to help blend. Strain.

Once the sauce is strained, warm the oil in a preheated Dutch oven or large skillet over medium-high heat. Once the oil is shimmering, add the sauce and quickly fry for 3 minutes, stirring constantly. Remove from the heat and season with salt and black pepper to taste, if desired.

Use immediately to make enchiladas, or set aside to cool. This sauce will keep in the refrigerator for up to 1 week and in the freezer for up to 1 month.

ENCHILADA VERDE SAUCE

I'm addicted to tomatillos and found myself buying loads of canned enchilada verde sauce at the supermarket. Then it hit me—why not make a big batch at home, where I can control the ingredients? Once it's made, I use some for dinner and then store the rest for future use. It freezes beautifully, so you'll always have homemade enchilada sauce on hand.

MAKES 6 TO 7 CUPS

4 pounds tomatillos, husked, rinsed, and sliced

4 cups chicken broth, plus more if needed

2 large onions, sliced

5 garlic cloves

1 bunch fresh cilantro leaves, coarsely chopped

1 tablespoon salt, plus more to taste

2 teaspoons freshly ground black pepper, plus more to taste

1½ teaspoons ground cumin

¼ cup freshly squeezed lime juice

Combine the tomatillos, 4 cups of the chicken broth, the onions, the garlic, the cilantro, 1 tablespoon of the salt, 2 teaspoons of the black pepper, and the cumin in a slow cooker. Cover and cook on low for 8 hours.

Carefully blend the cooked enchilada sauce with an immersion blender or in batches using a blender until smooth; add more chicken broth (½ cup at a time) if needed. Stir in the lime juice and season with salt and black pepper to taste, if desired.

Use immediately to make an Enchilada Casserole (page 75) or set aside to cool to room temperature. This sauce will keep in the refrigerator for up to 1 week and in the freezer for up to 1 month.

NOTE: ENCHILADA SAUCE BECOMES THICKER AS IT COOLS; USE WATER OR CHICKEN BROTH TO THIN IT TO THE DESIRED CONSISTENCY.

MOLE SAUCE

Making mole can be an all-day event, once you consider everything from grinding the spices to preparing the chiles. As much as we enjoy having mole for dinner, I decided it was time to pull out my slow cooker and create an easier recipe. This rich, chocolatey mole sauce can be used for Mole Tacos (page 81), Mole Nachos (page 31), or simply served warm over poached chicken.

MAKES 6 CUPS

4 dried ancho chiles, stems and seeds removed

Water to cover

4 cups chicken broth

3 corn tostada shells (see note)

1 onion, sliced

¼ cup plus 3 tablespoons peanut butter

3 garlic cloves, minced

1 Mexican chocolate tablet (I prefer Abuelita or Ibarra brands)

1 teaspoon ground cumin

1 teaspoon dried oregano

1 teaspoon salt

1 teaspoon freshly ground black pepper

Place the chiles in a microwave-safe bowl, cover with water, and microwave on high 5 minutes. Remove from the microwave, cover, and set aside to steep for 5 minutes.

Drain the chiles and place them in a slow cooker, along with all of the remaining ingredients. Cover and cook on low for 6 hours.

Carefully blend the cooked Mole Sauce with an immersion blender or in batches using a blender until smooth. Season with additional salt and black pepper to taste, if desired, and serve.

If keeping warm, return the blended sauce to the slow cooker and reduce the setting to warm. If storing for later use, allow to cool completely and store in the refrigerator for up to 1 week. Mole Sauce can also be frozen for up to 3 months.

NOTE: YOU CAN BAKE OR FRY CORN TORTILLAS TO MAKE YOUR OWN TOSTADAS, BUT TO SAVE TIME, I USE STORE-BOUGHT TOSTADA SHELLS.

PICO DE GALLO

A fresh salsa made with tomatoes, onions, and plenty of jalapeños, *pico de gallo* is widely popular here in South Texas. You don't need a slow cooker for this recipe, but it's so delicious I had to include it. Spooned over any of the tacos in this book or eggs or served with tortilla chips, *pico de gallo* is a welcome sight at any get-together.

Makes 2 cups

4 tomatoes, diced

1 small onion, diced

2 jalapeño peppers, diced (remove and discard the seeds for less heat)

¼ cup chopped fresh cilantro

Freshly squeezed juice of 1 lime

Salt and freshly ground black pepper to taste

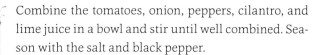

Combine the tomatoes, onion, peppers, cilantro, and lime juice in a bowl and stir until well combined. Season with the salt and black pepper.

Store in a sealed container in the refrigerator for up to 2 days until ready to serve.

ELOTE RICE

In this recipe, I transform one of my favorite snacks into a yummy side dish. *Elote*, a popular street food in Mexico, is a corn cob on a stick covered in *crema*, *queso fresco*, chiles, and lime. This *elote* rice is loaded with all of the delicious flavors of Mexico.

SERVES 4

1 (15¼-ounce) can corn, drained

1½ cups chicken broth

1 cup uncooked white rice

½ cup Mexican *crema*

1 tablespoon unsalted butter

1 teaspoon salt

1 teaspoon freshly ground black pepper

¼ cup freshly squeezed lime juice

½ cup crumbled *queso fresco* and ground ancho chile, for garnish

Liberally spray a slow-cooker liner with nonstick cooking spray. Add the corn, broth, rice, *crema*, butter, salt, and black pepper and stir until well combined. Cover and cook on high for 2 hours.

After 2 hours, check the rice for doneness, as slow cookers' temperatures can vary. If the rice is not done, reduce the setting to low and cook for 30 more minutes.

Fluff the rice with a fork and add the lime juice. Garnish with the *queso fresco* and ancho chile and serve warm.

MEXICAN RICE

Every great Tex-Mex combination plate is always accompanied by a hefty serving of Mexican rice. My version features fresh chiles, which give this rice an extra kick of flavor. If you love a little spice, you'll love this recipe.

SERVES 4

2 cups uncooked white rice

2 cups chicken broth

1 (15-ounce) can Mexican-style diced tomatoes

¼ cup diced onion

1 teaspoon salt

½ teaspoon freshly ground black pepper

½ teaspoon ground cumin

1 serrano chile, thinly sliced (optional; remove the seeds for less heat)

¼ cup freshly squeezed lime juice

Lime wedges and ¼ cup chopped fresh cilantro, for garnish

Liberally spray a slow-cooker liner with nonstick cooking spray. Add the rice, broth, tomatoes, onion, salt, black pepper, cumin, and serrano chile, if using, and stir until well combined. Cover and cook on high for 2 hours.

After 2 hours, check the rice for doneness, as slow cookers' temperatures can vary. If the rice is not done, reduce the setting to low and cook for 30 more minutes.

Fluff the rice with a fork and add the lime juice. Serve warm garnished with the lime wedges and cilantro.

FRIJOLES DE LA OLLA

When I was growing up, my *mami* made a batch of *frijoles de la olla* every Monday to use in meals all throughout the week. The smell of beans slowly cooking away on the stove reminds me of my childhood. Now, as a *mami* myself, I make beans every Monday, just like her, but I like to let my slow cooker do the work. These frijoles are the perfect base for Charro Beans (page 107), or they can be used to make refried beans. Have leftovers? Simply freeze them for another meal. Thaw the beans overnight in the fridge when ready to use.

Serves 8 to 10

1 pound dried pinto beans

½ onion, diced

4 garlic cloves

2 bay leaves

Water to cover

Salt to taste

Chopped fresh cilantro, diced tomatoes, and Mexican *crema* or *queso fresco*, for serving

Wash and pick through the beans, removing any bits of debris or broken beans, and place them in a bowl. Repeatedly rinse and drain the beans under cold water until the water runs clear. Drain.

Combine the beans, onion, bay leaves, and garlic in a slow cooker and add enough water to cover the beans by at least 2 inches. Cover and cook on low for 6 to 8 hours.

After 3 hours, check the beans for doneness, as slow cookers' temperatures can vary. If the beans are not done, continue cooking. Add more water, if needed; there should be at least 2 inches of water covering the beans at all times. This will help the beans to cook more evenly. When done, the beans should be soft, but not mushy or falling apart. When the beans are done, remove and discard the onion and bay leaves and season to taste with the salt.

Serve warm in large bowls garnished with the cilantro, tomatoes, and *crema*, or a sprinkle of the *queso fresco*.

BORRACHO BEANS

These pinto beans are cooked low and slow for 7 hours in a rich beer broth and studded with crispy bacon, tomatoes, jalapeños, and onions. These *borracho* beans are the ultimate party fare, served alongside a big *molcajete* (mortar and pestle) of guacamole or with a stack of warm corn tortillas.

SERVES 8 TO 10

1 pound dried pinto beans

1 (12-ounce) can beer

2 garlic cloves

Water to cover

1 pound thick-cut bacon

1 medium onion, chopped

3 fresh Roma tomatoes, diced, or 1 (15-ounce) can diced tomatoes

2 jalapeño peppers, chopped (optional)

½ teaspoon ground cumin

Salt and freshly ground black pepper to taste

Chopped fresh cilantro, for garnish

Wash and pick through the beans, removing any bits of debris or broken beans, and place them in a bowl. Repeatedly rinse and drain the beans under cold water until the water runs clear. Drain.

Combine the beans, beer, and garlic in a slow cooker and add enough water to cover the beans by at least 2 inches. Cover and cook on low for 6 to 8 hours.

After 3 hours, check the beans for doneness, as slow cookers' temperatures can vary. If the beans are not done, continue cooking. Add more water, if needed; there should be at least 2 inches of water covering the beans at all times. This will help the beans to cook more evenly. When done, the beans should be soft, but not mushy or falling apart. Reduce the setting to warm.

Warm a nonstick skillet over medium-high heat. Add the bacon and cook until crisp. Remove the bacon from the pan and place it on a paper towel–lined plate to drain.

Add the onions to the skillet and cook, stirring frequently to loosen the brown bits left behind in the pan from the bacon, for 2 to 3 minutes. Add the tomatoes and jalapeños (if using) and, cook, continuing to stir and incorporate any leftover bits from the skillet, keeping all of that delicious goodness in your beans, for 2 to 3 minutes. Remove from the heat.

Add the contents of the skillet to the beans, along with the cooked bacon Add the cumin and season to taste with the salt and black pepper. Stir until well combined.

Garnish with the cilantro and serve warm.

CHARRO BEANS

I've always said that I could live off beans for the rest of my life. These *charro* beans are my ultimate "last meal." In Texas, *charro* beans, also known as "cowboy beans," can be found in just about every Tex-Mex joint, served in little bowls alongside your meal. There are many, many different versions of this recipe, and this is my own take on *charro* beans.

SERVES 8 TO 10 AS A MEAL OR MORE IF SERVED AS A SIDE DISH

1 recipe Frijoles de la Olla (page 104)
8 slices bacon, diced
1 pound fully cooked sausage, sliced
1 medium onion, chopped
2 to 3 tomatoes, chopped
2 serrano peppers, thinly sliced (optional)
2 garlic cloves, finely chopped
Salt and freshly ground black pepper to taste
Chopped fresh cilantro leaves, for garnish

Prepare the Frijoles de Olla recipe.

When the *frijoles* are almost done, warm a nonstick skillet over medium-high heat. Add the bacon and cook until crisp. Remove the bacon from the pan with a slotted spoon and place it on a paper towel–lined plate to drain.

Add the sausage to the skillet and cook for 2 minutes, or until it crisps slightly. Take care not to crowd the pan; work in batches if necessary. Remove the sausage from the pan with a slotted spoon and place it on a paper towel–lined plate to drain.

Add the onion to the skillet and sauté, stirring constantly to release the brown bits from the pan, for 2 minutes. Add the tomatoes, serranos (if using), and garlic and continue to sauté for 3 minutes. Remove from the heat and season with the salt and black pepper.

Add the cooked bacon and sausage and the contents of the skillet to the slow cooker containing the beans; reduce the setting to warm. Stir until well combined and season with more salt and black pepper, if desired. Serve warm, garnished with the cilantro.

CHEESY JALAPEÑO CORN BREAD

All hail the mighty Texas corn bread. Served alongside beans or chili, or made into stuffing, corn bread is always a hit at any Texas table. I've taken the traditional corn bread recipe and given it a Tex-Mex twist by adding *masa harina* to the batter, plus plenty of pickled jalapeños and Cheddar. The *masa harina* gives it a depth of flavor, while the Cheddar cubes melt into little pockets of cheesy goodness. If you can't find *masa harina* in the Latin section of your grocery store, use all-purpose flour instead.

MAKES 1 LOAF

1 cup yellow cornmeal

¾ cup *masa harina* (I recommend Maseca)

1 tablespoon baking powder

1 teaspoon salt

1 cup whole milk

2 large eggs, lightly beaten

¼ cup vegetable oil

¼ cup sliced pickled jalapeño peppers

1 cup cubed Cheddar

Lightly coat a slow cooker with nonstick cooking spray.

Whisk together the dry ingredients—the cornmeal, *masa harina*, baking powder, and salt—in a large bowl and set aside. In a second, smaller bowl, whisk together the wet ingredients—the milk, eggs, and oil. Stir the pickled jalapeños into the wet ingredients.

Gradually add the wet ingredients to the dry ingredients in the larger bowl and stir until well combined.

Pour the corn bread batter into a slow cooker and spread the top with the back of a spoon to smooth it out. Then, individually add the cheese cubes on top, lightly pressing each cube into the batter. Cover and cook on high for 1½ to 2 hours.

After 1½ hours, check the corn bread by inserting a toothpick or knife. If it comes out clean, the bread is ready; if not, continue to cook for 30 minutes.

Carefully remove the liner from the slow cooker to stop the cooking process. Set aside to cool for 15 minutes and then run a knife around the edges to loosen the corn bread. Serve warm.

ROASTED POBLANO-CHORIZO MAC AND CHEESE

This mac-and-cheese recipe is for the grown-ups. Studded with roasted poblanos, chorizo, and plenty of cheese, this recipe is sure to satisfy all your Tex-Mex cravings. The topping, made with a mix of Maria cookies and cilantro, adds a touch of sweetness to this side dish. I could eat the entire batch myself.

SERVES 8 TO 10

1 poblano pepper

1 pound elbow macaroni

4 cups shredded Cheddar

2 (12-ounce) cans evaporated milk

2 cups whole milk

1 teaspoon salt

½ teaspoon garlic powder

8 ounces chorizo sausage, fully cooked

½ cup chopped fresh cilantro leaves

4 Maria cookies or saltine crackers, broken into pieces

Preheat the broiler and place the poblano on a baking sheet.

Broil the poblano for 4 to 6 minutes on each side, or until it is charred on all sides. Remove from the oven, cover with a dish towel, and set aside to steam for about 5 minutes.

Remove and discard the poblano's charred skin, stems, and seeds and dice the pepper. Set aside.

Combine the diced poblano, macaroni, cheese, evaporated milk, whole milk, salt, and garlic powder in the slow cooker and stir until well combined. Cover and cook on low for 2½ to 3 hours.

After 2½ hours, check the macaroni for doneness, as slow cookers' temperatures can vary. If the macaroni is still soupy, continue cooking for an additional 30 minutes. When the macaroni is done, all of the liquid should be absorbed.

Carefully remove the liner from the slow cooker to stop the cooking process. Stir the chorizo into the mixture.

Combine the cilantro and broken cookies in a small bowl and scatter it on the top of the mixture. Serve warm.

RAJAS CON CREMA MASHED POTATOES

When I was growing up, every year after Thanksgiving, *mi mami* would use leftover mashed potatoes to make potato tacos: mashed potatoes stuffed into a crispy taco shell and fried until golden brown. She would serve these tacos with *rajas con crema* and plenty of finely shredded cabbage. I've taken the best of both worlds and made this recipe: my dream mashed potatoes. Made in the slow cooker, this is the ultimate savory side dish.

SERVES 8 TO 10

3 poblano peppers

5 pounds potatoes, peeled and cut into chunks (russet works best)

1½ cups chicken broth

4 tablespoons (½ stick) unsalted butter

3 garlic cloves

1 teaspoon salt, plus more if needed

½ cup Mexican *crema*

½ cup whole milk

Freshly ground black pepper

Queso fresco, for garnish

Preheat the broiler and place the poblanos on a baking sheet.

Broil the poblanos for 4 to 6 minutes on each side, or until they are charred on all sides. Remove from the oven, cover with a dish towel, and set aside to steam for about 5 minutes.

Remove and discard the poblanos' charred skin, stems, and seeds and slice the peppers into strips.

Combine the potatoes, chicken broth, butter, garlic, and salt in a slow cooker and stir until well combined. Cover and cook on low for 4 to 5 hours.

After 4 hours, check the potatoes by piercing them with a fork. They are done when a fork goes through easily, but they are not mushy. If they are not done, continue cooking and checking at 20-minute intervals for doneness.

Add the *crema* and the milk, a little at a time, while mashing constantly with a potato masher until you reach the desired consistency. Season with the salt, if needed, and the black pepper. Stir in the strips of roasted poblanos and serve warm garnished with the *queso fresco*.

HOMINY SQUASH CASSEROLE

I'll find any excuse to add my beloved hominy to a dish. Traditionally added to *menudo* or *pozole*, this humble treasure should be highlighted more. I also add plenty of squash, diced tomatoes, and *crema* to my hominy in this recipe, creating a homey hominy casserole.

SERVES 4 TO 6

1 pound squash, diced

1 (15-ounce) can hominy

1 (15-ounce) can Mexican style
 diced tomatoes

½ cup diced onion

1 teaspoon salt

1 teaspoon freshly ground black
 pepper

¼ teaspoon dried oregano

1½ to 2 cups chicken broth

1 cup shredded Cheddar, plus
 more for garnish

¼ cup Mexican *crema*

½ cup chopped fresh cilantro
 leaves, for garnish

 Combine the squash, hominy, tomatoes, onion, salt, black pepper, and oregano in a slow cooker. Gradually add 1½ cups of the chicken broth to the mixture; the mixture should be covered by the broth, but there shouldn't be so much broth that it doesn't fully absorb, creating a casserole consistency. Add the remaining ½ cup of the broth, if needed.

Add 1 cup of the cheese and the *crema* and stir until all the ingredients are well combined. Cover and cook on low for 4 hours.

After 4 hours, check the squash to see if all of the broth has been absorbed, as slow cookers' temperatures can vary. If the broth has not been completely absorbed, continue cooking and checking at 20-minute intervals for doneness.

Once all the broth has been absorbed, garnish with the remaining cheese and the cilantro and serve warm.

CREAMY NOPAL RICE

My mother-in-law grows an abundance of *nopales* in her front yard. She knows my love of cooking, so she keeps me stocked with them at all times. I scramble them into eggs for breakfast, add them to queso, and use them in stews. I recently added them to rice, and the results were amazing. Since you can never have enough rice dishes to serve alongside amazing enchiladas, I've created a delicious version featuring *nopales*. No need to worry about cleaning those pesky cactus paddles—for this recipe, I use jarred *nopales*. Shhh—don't tell my mother-in law. *Besotes*, Minnie.

Serves 4

1½ cups *nopales*, jarred or canned
1½ cups chicken broth
1 cup uncooked white rice
½ cup Mexican *crema*
1 tablespoon unsalted butter
1 teaspoon salt
1 teaspoon freshly ground black
  pepper
¼ cup freshly squeezed lime juice
¼ cup minced fresh cilantro
  leaves, for garnish
Salsa Verde (page 92), for serving

Liberally spray a slow-cooker liner with nonstick cooking spray. Add the *nopales*, broth, rice, *crema*, butter, salt, and black pepper and stir until well combined. Cook on high for 2 hours and then reduce the setting to low and continue to cook for an additional 30 minutes.

After 2½ hours, check the rice for doneness, as slow cookers' temperatures can vary. If all of the liquid has not yet been absorbed, continue cooking and checking at 10-minute intervals for doneness.

Fluff the rice with a fork and add the lime juice. Garnish with the cilantro and serve warm with the Salsa Verde.

DESSERTS

DULCE DE LECHE CHOCOLATE CAKE
WITH STRAWBERRY SAUCE 120

PEACH-PECAN UPSIDE-DOWN CAKE 123

STRAWBERRY-PILONCILLO ICE CREAM SAUCE 124

CAPIROTADA 127

CHOCOLATE-PECAN TEXAS SHEET CAKE 128

VALLEY LEMON CAKE 131

MEXICAN CHOCOLATE PAN DULCE BREAD PUDDING 132

CHURRO BITES WITH CHOCOLATE SAUCE 135

MEXICAN CHOCOLATE GRANOLA 136

PUMPKIN-CINNAMON FRENCH TOAST 139

ATOLE DE AVENA 140

DULCE DE LECHE CHOCOLATE CAKE WITH STRAWBERRY SAUCE

MAKE IN A 4-QUART SLOW COOKER

My daughters are addicted to dulce de leche, so it often makes an appearance in our desserts. This dreamy, creamy cake is rich and decadent. I top it off with a sweet and tart strawberry sauce—voilà, an instant family favorite!

SERVES 6 TO 8

2 cups strawberries, hulled and sliced

1 tablespoon granulated sugar

1 tablespoon freshly squeezed lemon juice

2 cups whole milk

1 (3.9-ounce) box instant chocolate pudding mix

1 (15¼-ounce) package chocolate cake mix

1 cup water

3 large eggs

⅓ cup vegetable oil

¼ cup warmed dulce de leche, plus more for garnish

Combine the strawberries, sugar, and lemon juice in a bowl and stir until well combined. Cover with plastic wrap and refrigerate until ready to serve with the cake.

Liberally spray a slow-cooker liner with nonstick cooking spray. Whisk together the milk and pudding mix in a small bowl and set aside.

In a second, larger bowl, stir together the cake mix, water, eggs, and vegetable oil until well combined. Add the pudding mixture to the cake batter and stir until just combined.

Transfer the batter to the slow cooker, spreading the top with the back of a spoon to ensure it is smooth and evenly distributed. Add ¼ cup of the dulce de leche in spoonfuls over the cake batter. Cover and cook on low for 4 hours or on high for 2 to 2½ hours. To check for doneness, insert a toothpick into the center of the cake; if it comes out clean, it is done.

Carefully remove the liner from the slow cooker to stop the cooking process. Serve warm topped with the chilled strawberry sauce and drizzled with more of the warm dulce de leche.

PEACH-PECAN UPSIDE-DOWN CAKE

Make in a 6-quart slow cooker

Pineapple upside-down cake was one of the first attempts I made at baking, and it was a complete disaster. Over the years, I've found that my slow cooker does a much better job. To make the recipe even easier, I use canned peaches and plenty of fragrant Texas pecans.

Serves 6 to 8

1 cup light brown sugar

¼ cup melted unsalted butter

2 (15-ounce) cans sliced peaches, drained and juice reserved

¼ cup pecan halves

1 (15¼-ounce) box yellow cake mix

3 large eggs

⅓ cup vegetable oil

1 teaspoon vanilla extract

1 cup heavy whipping cream beaten together with 2 tablespoons granulated sugar (see note), for topping

Liberally spray a slow cooker with nonstick cooking spray.

Using a fork, stir together the brown sugar and butter in a small bowl and transfer the mixture into a slow cooker. Arrange the peaches evenly over the brown sugar layer, starting at the exterior of the slow-cooker liner and working toward the middle. Add the pecans, pushing them in just slightly between the peach slices.

Stir together the cake mix, 1 cup of the reserved peach juice, the eggs, the oil, and the vanilla in a bowl. Transfer the batter to the slow cooker, spreading the top with the back of a spoon to ensure it is smooth and evenly distributed. Cover and cook on low for 4 hours or on high for 2 to 2½ hours. To check for doneness, insert a toothpick into the center of the cake; if it comes out clean, it is done.

Carefully remove the liner from the slow cooker to stop the cooking process. Serve warm topped with the whipped cream.

Note: To make the whipped cream, beat together the heavy cream and sugar until light and fluffy.

STRAWBERRY-PILONCILLO ICE CREAM SAUCE

MAKE IN A 4-QUART SLOW COOKER

Ohh, the sweet south Texas heat. Temperatures that rise into the 90s, with plenty of humidity, call for ice cream. This strawberry sauce, which is made with *piloncillo,* is my family's topping of choice. To get more use out of it, drizzle it over pancakes or waffles.

MAKES 4 CUPS

2 pounds frozen strawberries

½ cup freshly grated *piloncillo* (see page 36) or light brown sugar

2 (4-inch) cinnamon sticks

Combine all of the ingredients in a slow cooker. Cover and cook on low for 4 hours, or until the berries break down into chunks. If you want a thinner sauce, cook for 1 hour more.

Remove and discard the cinnamon sticks and set aside to cool completely. Drizzle over ice cream, cakes, or pancakes.

CAPIROTADA

Make in a 4-quart slow cooker

Capirotada, a favorite Lenten recipe, is widely popular in Texas. The dish consists of layers of toasted bread, spiced syrup, dried fruit, nuts, and plenty of cheese. All the ingredients combine to create the perfect crisp, yet tender bread pudding.

Serves 6 to 8

6 *bolillos*, torn into pieces (see note)

4 cups water

2 *piloncillo* cones (see page 36), freshly grated, or 2 cups light brown sugar

2 (4-inch) cinnamon sticks

4 whole cloves

1 star anise

2 cups shredded Cheddar

1 cup raisins

1 cup chopped pecans or walnuts, plus more for garnish

Preheat the oven to 350°F.

Spread out the *bolillo* pieces on a baking sheet and bake for 5 to 8 minutes, or until lightly browned and toasted. Remove from the oven and set aside to cool.

Combine the water, *piloncillo*, cinnamon sticks, cloves, and star anise in a large saucepan over medium-high heat. Bring to a boil, reduce heat to low, and simmer for 10 minutes. Remove from the heat and strain into a bowl. (The syrup can be made a day in advance.)

Liberally spray a slow-cooker liner with nonstick cooking spray. Place half of the *bolillo* pieces in the slow cooker and add half of each of the cheese, the raisins, and the 1 cup of the pecans. Add a second layer of the remaining *bolillo* pieces and add the remaining raisins and pecans, finishing with the remaining cheese. Top with the cooled syrup and then press down on the pieces with the back of a spoon, ensuring they are fully submerged. Cover and cook for low for 4 hours or on high for 2 hours, or until all of the syrup is absorbed and the center is set.

Reduce the setting to warm and serve warm garnished with more of the pecans.

Note: A *bolillo* is a roll typically served with meals in Mexico. With crusty exteriors and soft interiors, *bolillos* are used to make *tortas*.

CHOCOLATE–PECAN TEXAS SHEET CAKE

MAKE IN A 6-QUART SLOW COOKER

Everything's bigger in Texas—even our cakes. Texas sheet cakes, which are traditionally made in a sheet pan, are a beloved potluck favorite. This variation on the classic is smaller and requires a few steps, but trust me, it's worth it! Studded with plenty of chocolate chips and roasted pecans, this Chocolate–Pecan Texas Sheet Cake is insanely delicious.

SERVES 6 TO 8

For the Cake:

¼ cup buttermilk

1 large egg

½ teaspoon vanilla extract

½ teaspoon baking soda

1 cup all-purpose flour

1 cup granulated sugar

½ teaspoon ground cinnamon

½ teaspoon salt

½ cup water

4 tablespoons (½ stick) unsalted butter

¼ cup shortening

3 tablespoons cocoa powder

Make the Cake:

Liberally spray a slow-cooker liner with nonstick cooking spray.

Whisk together the buttermilk, egg, vanilla, and baking soda in a small bowl. In a second, larger bowl, mix together the flour, sugar, cinnamon, and salt.

Combine the water, butter, shortening, and cocoa powder in a saucepan over medium-high heat and bring to a boil, stirring occasionally until combined. Remove from the heat and pour over the flour mixture, stirring until well incorporated. Slowly add the buttermilk mixture to the larger bowl, stirring until all of the ingredients are well incorporated.

Pour the cake batter into the slow cooker. Cover and cook on low for 3 to 4 hours. To check for doneness, insert a toothpick into the center of the cake; if it comes out clean, it is done.

Carefully remove the liner from the slow cooker to stop the cooking process. Cover and set aside.

For the Glaze:

- 4 tablespoons (½ stick) unsalted butter
- 3 tablespoons buttermilk
- 3 tablespoons cocoa powder
- 2 cups confectioners' sugar
- 1 cup pecan halves, for garnish

Make the Glaze:

Combine the butter, buttermilk, and cocoa powder in a saucepan over medium-high heat and bring to a boil, stirring occasionally until combined. Remove from the heat and whisk in the confectioners' sugar until the mixture is smooth.

Pour the glaze over the warm cake and serve garnished with the pecans.

VALLEY LEMON CAKE

Valley lemons flourish in the Rio Grande Valley—hence their name. They are plump, juicy, and completely addictive; I buy them by the 10-pound bag. Used in cocktails, marinades, cakes, and puddings, Valley lemons are a classic south Texas treasure.

SERVES 6 TO 8

For the Cake:

1 (15¼-ounce) box yellow cake mix

3 large eggs

½ cup water

½ cup Valley lemon or regular freshly squeezed lemon or lime juice

⅓ cup vegetable oil

2 teaspoons freshly grated Valley lemon or regular lemon zest

For the Glaze:

1 cup confectioners' sugar

2 tablespoons Valley lemon or regular freshly squeezed lemon or lime juice

1 thinly sliced Valley or regular lemon, for garnish

Make the Cake:

Liberally spray a slow-cooker liner with nonstick cooking spray.

Combine the cake mix, eggs, water, lemon juice, oil, and lemon zest in a bowl and stir until well combined.

Transfer the batter to the slow cooker. Cover and cook on high for 2 to 2½ hours. To check for doneness, insert a toothpick into the center of the cake; if it comes out clean, it is done.

Reduce the setting to warm.

Make the Glaze:

Whisk together the confectioners' sugar and lemon juice in a small bowl until smooth.

Pour the glaze over the warm cake. Serve warm garnished with the lemon slices.

MEXICAN CHOCOLATE PAN DULCE BREAD PUDDING

My family is addicted to *conchas*: they're light, fluffy, and oh-so-sweet. *Pan dulce* is our go-to Sunday morning treat; that's why I knew my family would love this super fun and special twist on classic bread pudding.

SERVES 6

2 cups whole milk

½ cup freshly grated *piloncillo* (see page 36)

2 (4-inch) cinnamon sticks

1 whole star anise

1 Mexican chocolate disc (I recommend Abuelita or Ibarra)

4 large eggs

8 *conchas* (see note), cut into cubes

1 cup slivered almonds

1 cup raisins

NOTE: CONCHAS ARE MEXICAN SWEET BREADS (*PAN DULCE*) THAT GET THEIR NAME FROM THE CRUMBLY SWEET TOPPING PLACED OVER THE BREAD IN A SHELL-LIKE PATTERN. IN ENGLISH, CONCHA MEANS "SHELL."

Liberally spray a slow-cooker liner with nonstick cooking spray.

Combine the milk, *piloncillo*, cinnamon, and star anise in a saucepan over medium heat and bring to a simmer. Immediately remove from the heat, remove and discard the cinnamon and star anise, and add the chocolate disc. Whisk vigorously until all of the chocolate dissolves. Set aside to cool completely.

Once the milk mixture is cool, add the eggs and whisk until well combined.

Place half of the *concha* cubes in a slow cooker and add half of each of the almonds and the raisins. Top with half of the milk mixture and then press down on the cubes with the back of a spoon, ensuring the cubes are fully submerged.

Add a second layer of the remaining *concha* cubes and add the remaining almonds and raisins. Top with the remaining milk mixture and then press down on the cubes with the back of a spoon, ensuring the cubes are fully submerged. Cover and cook for low for 4 hours, or until all of the milk is absorbed and the center is set. Serve warm.

CHURRO BITES WITH CHOCOLATE SAUCE

MAKE IN A 4-QUART SLOW COOKER

I adore churros, but I have no desire to be tied down to the fryer as I fry them up, one at a time. I'd rather take a few shortcuts with this recipe and savor the richness of churros soaked in chocolate drizzle with half the effort.

SERVES 6 TO 8

For the Churros:

1 cup granulated sugar

2 tablespoons ground cinnamon

4 (7½-ounce) tubes refrigerated biscuit dough

½ cup melted unsalted butter

For the Chocolate Sauce:

12 ounces semisweet or dark chocolate

12 ounces heavy cream

Make the Churros:

Liberally spray a slow-cooker liner with nonstick cooking spray.

Combine the sugar and cinnamon in a large, shallow mixing bowl and set aside.

Remove the biscuit dough from the packaging and cut each biscuit into fourths. Coat each biscuit piece with the butter and then with the cinnamon–sugar mixture. Place each coated biscuit piece in the slow cooker; continue this process until all are in the slow cooker.

Cover and cook on high for 2 to 2½ hours, or until a toothpick inserted into a biscuit comes out clean.

Make the Chocolate Sauce:

Combine the ingredients in a microwave-safe bowl and microwave on high for 1 minute. Carefully remove the bowl from the microwave and whisk until smooth. If the chocolate is still too thick, return to the microwave and cook on high in 30-second increments until the desired consistency is reached.

Serve with the warm churro bites.

MEXCIAN CHOCOLATE GRANOLA

When I was pregnant with my second child, I was obsessed with granola—I ate it for breakfast, as a snack, and again as a midnight snack. I soon found that by making my own, I could customize my granola with all my favorite flavors. This granola, which is sweetened with agave, is brimming with pecans, pepitas, and plenty of Mexican chocolate.

SERVES 12

5 cups old-fashioned (not quick-cooking) oats

2 cups pecan halves

2 cups unsalted pepitas (pumpkin seeds), roasted

2 (3-ounce) Mexican chocolate discs (I recommend Abuelita), freshly grated

1 cup agave syrup

½ cup canola oil

Whole milk or plain yogurt, for serving

Combine the oats, pecans, pepitas, and chocolate in a slow cooker and stir together the ingredients.

Whisk together the agave and oil in a small bowl and pour it over the oat mixture. Stir until well coated. Cover and cook, stirring every 30 minutes, on high for 2 hours or low for 4 hours.

Serve warm with the milk or set aside to cool completely and serve with the yogurt. The granola will keep at room temperature stored in an airtight container for up to 1 month.

PUMPKIN-CINNAMON FRENCH TOAST

My oldest daughter loves baking with pumpkin. Everything from bread to muffins to French toast—she sneaks pumpkin into many of her baked goods. This slow-cooker French toast recipe was her idea. Made with lightly toasted Texas toast and plenty of pumpkin, this has quickly become our favorite go-to lazy-Sunday brunch fare, since our slow cooker does all the work.

SERVES 6 TO 8

1 loaf Texas toast (see note), cut into cubes

2 cups whole milk

6 large eggs

1 cup canned pumpkin puree

½ cup light brown sugar

¼ cup melted unsalted butter

1 teaspoon ground cinnamon

1 teaspoon vanilla extract

½ teaspoon ground nutmeg

1 cup pecan halves, plus more for serving

Maple syrup, for serving

Preheat the oven to 400°F. Liberally spray a slow-cooker liner with nonstick cooking spray.

Place the Texas toast cubes on a baking sheet and bake, stirring halfway through the baking time, for 5 to 10 minutes, or until lightly toasted. (This can be done up to a day in advance.)

Place the toasted bread cubes in the slow cooker.

Whisk together the milk, eggs, pumpkin, brown sugar, butter, cinnamon, vanilla, and nutmeg in a large bowl until smooth. Pour the mixture over the toasted bread cubes, stirring until all are fully coated. Cover and cook on low for 4 hours.

Serve warm with the pecans and warm maple syrup.

NOTE: TEXAS TOAST, WHICH IS SAID TO HAVE BEEN INVENTED IN BEAUMONT, TEXAS, IS BREAD SLICED AT DOUBLE THE THICKNESS OF A REGULAR SLICE OF BREAD. IT CAN BE FOUND THROUGHOUT TEXAS; TO SUBSTITUTE, BAKE OR BUY A WHOLE UNSLICED LOAF OF BREAD AND SLICE IT UP YOURSELF.

ATOLE DE AVENA

When the days became shorter and the mornings were chilly, my mother would make us *avena* before we headed out to school. This milky oatmeal laced with cinnamon and *piloncillo* served in a coffee mug was the perfect way to soothe us before a long day in class. I always felt a bit more grown up sipping my *avena* from a coffee cup next to my dad, while he sipped his morning coffee. The thick, steamy *avena* would hit your *pancita* (belly)—just the thing to hold you over until lunchtime. This creamy oatmeal dish can be cooked in the slow cooker overnight.

SERVES 4

3 cups whole milk

2 cups old-fashioned oats

2 cups water

¼ cup freshly grated *piloncillo*
   (see page 36) or light brown
   sugar, plus more for serving

1 (4-inch) Mexican cinnamon stick

¼ teaspoon salt

Combine the milk, oats, water, ¼ cup *piloncillo*, cinnamon stick, and salt in a slow cooker. Cover and cook on low for 8 hours. Remove and discard the cinnamon stick and serve warm with more of the *piloncillo*.

BEVERAGES AND COCKTAILS

SIMPLE SYRUPS

When it comes to cocktailing at home, I prefer to make my own simple syrups—they taste better than store-bought versions, and they don't contain any fillers or additives. I always have homemade simple syrup on hand, plus a few seasonal variations that make shaking up cocktails a breeze. My family and friends love my homemade simple syrups and often ask me to make them a few bottles of their own.

LAVENDER SYRUP

Every year, we attend the Blanco Lavender Festival in Blanco, Texas. We head into the fields to pick fresh lavender, sip on our favorite lavender lemonade, and buy plenty of dried lavender. I use lavender to make everything from breads to sauces and even cocktails. Ya'll know how much I love to use simple, natural ingredients. Well, this Lavender Syrup is the real deal. There's no dye or other additives—just pure, simple lavender essence, locally sourced from Blanco, Texas. Use it to quickly whip up cocktails, mocktails, coolers, or lemonade.

MAKES 6 CUPS

6 cups water
3 cups granulated sugar
1 cup ground dried lavender

Combine the water, sugar, and lavender in a slow cooker and stir until well combined. Cover and cook on low for 4 hours.

Allow the syrup to cool completely before pouring it into a clean storage bottle; straining is optional, as you can leave some lavender in the bottle. Lavender Syrup will keep for up to 1 month in a sealed container stored in the refrigerator and can be used to make cocktails or lemonade, or used to mix with tea.

HIBISCUS SYRUP

Hibiscus is one of my favorite ingredients. Its bold, intense flavor adds richness to some of my favorite sweet recipes. Whether I mix it into my favorite cocktails, drizzle it over ice cream, add it to *raspas* (shaved ice), or stir it into iced tea, it's a constant favorite.

MAKES 6 CUPS

6 cups water

4 cups freshly grated *piloncillo* (see page 36)

3 cups dried hibiscus flowers

Combine the water, *piloncillo*, and dried hibiscus in a slow cooker and stir until well combined. Cover and cook on low for 4 hours.

Allow the syrup to cool completely before straining it into a clean storage bottle. Hibiscus Syrup will keep for up to 1 month in a sealed container stored in the refrigerator and can be used to make cocktails or lemonade, or used to mix with tea.

CINNAMON SYRUP

My *abuelito* used to bring huge bundles of Mexican cinnamon when he would visit us in Texas. *Mi mami* would use it to make *te de canela* (cinnamon tea). Growing up, you could always find a pot of cinnamon tea on her stovetop. This cinnamon syrup reminds me of her kitchen and takes me back to so many great memories of growing up in south Texas.

MAKES 6 CUPS

6 cups water

3 cups granulated sugar

10 (4-inch) cinnamon sticks
  (see note)

Combine the water, sugar, and cinnamon sticks in a slow cooker and stir until well combined. Cover and cook on low for 4 hours.

Allow the syrup to cool completely before straining it into a clean storage bottle. Cinnamon Syrup will keep for up to 1 month in a sealed container stored in the refrigerator and can be used to make cocktails or lemonade, or used to mix with coffee or tea.

NOTE: I RECOMMEND USING MEXICAN CINNAMON STICKS FOR THIS RECIPE.

STRAWBERRY SYRUP

When I visit the Poteet Strawberry Festival, I scoop up as many pounds of fresh strawberries as I can get my greedy little hands on. They grow the best strawberries there! You can get everything from strawberry bread to strawberry cake to strawberry lemonade; the Poteet Strawberry Festival is a strawberry lover's delight. This dreamy Strawberry Syrup was inspired by our visits there.

MAKES 8 CUPS

3 pounds strawberries, hulled
   and sliced

8 cups water

3 cups granulated sugar

Combine the strawberries, water, and sugar in a slow cooker and stir until well combined. Cover and cook on low for 4 to 5 hours, or until the strawberries break down.

Mash the strawberries with a potato masher to release more of their intense flavor into the syrup.

Allow the syrup to cool completely before straining it into a clean storage bottle. Strawberry Syrup will keep for up to 2 weeks in a sealed container stored in the refrigerator and can be used to make cocktails or lemonade, or used to mix with tea.

NOTE: THE STRAINED-OUT STRAWBERRIES CAN BE USED TO TOP ICE CREAM, GRANOLA, OR YOGURT; BLENDED INTO MARGARITAS; OR USED TO MAKE *PALETAS*.

PECAN SYRUP

Evidence suggests that pecan trees grew in Texas since prehistoric times. By 1914, all but eight Texas counties hosted pecan trees. To say that Texans love pecans is an understatement—we can't get enough of them. After all, the pecan tree is Texas's state tree. My homemade Pecan Syrup will bring the essence of Texas straight to your table.

MAKES 6 CUPS

4 cups pecan halves

6 cups water

3 cups granulated sugar

Preheat the oven to 350ºF.

Place the pecans on a baking sheet and toast, stirring once, for 5 to 7 minutes. Remove from the oven.

Transfer the toasted pecans to a slow cooker and add the water and sugar. Cover and cook on low for 4 hours.

Allow the syrup to cool completely before straining it into a clean storage bottle. Pecan Syrup will keep for up to 2 weeks in a sealed container stored in the refrigerator and can be used to make cocktails or lemonade, used to mix with tea, or drizzled over a sheet cake.

NOTE: THE STRAINED-OUT PECANS CAN BE USED AS A TOPPING FOR ICE CREAM OR OATMEAL.

PEACH SYRUP

The idea for this syrup came after a weekend of peach-picking in Fredericksburg, Texas. We loaded up the kids and our dogs and headed out, and that weekend, we ate almost as much as we picked. We were sticky, sweaty, and completely stuffed. To this day, it's still one of our favorite family traditions; we go peach-picking in Fredericksburg every year.

MAKES 8 CUPS

3 pounds peaches, sliced and pitted

8 cups water

3 cups granulated sugar

Combine the peaches, water, and sugar in a slow cooker and stir until well combined. Cover and cook on low for 4 to 5 hours.

Mash the peaches with a potato masher to release more of their intense flavor into the syrup.

Allow the syrup to cool completely before straining it into a clean storage bottle. Peach Syrup will keep for up to 2 weeks in a sealed container stored in the refrigerator and can be used to make cocktails or lemonade, or used to mix with tea.

NOTE: THE STRAINED-OUT PEACHES CAN BE USED TO TOP ICE CREAM, BLENDED INTO MARGARITAS, OR USED TO MAKE *PALETAS.*

LAVENDER MARTINI

My Lavender Martini cocktail begins with a base of my homemade Lavender Syrup, which has become a necessity during the hot Texas summers. This delicious floral martini is a welcome treat on a hot day and is guaranteed to become a favorite new cocktail of your own!

MAKES 1 COCKTAIL

Ice

1 ounce vodka

½ ounce freshly squeezed lemon juice

¼ ounce Lavender Syrup (page 145)

Lemon slice, for garnish

Fill a cocktail shaker with ice and add the vodka, lemon juice, and Lavender Syrup. Shake well. Strain into a martini glass and serve garnished with a lemon slice.

STRAWBERRY LEMONADE

Texas summers can be brutal for our visiting friends, so I'm always sure to keep plenty of this Strawberry Lemonade on hand to quench their intense thirst. For a fun, adults-only version, add a splash of vodka to the mix.

SERVES 10 TO 12

6 cups fresh lemonade

2 cups Strawberry Syrup (page 148), plus more as needed

Ice

5 strawberries, sliced, for garnish

Stir together the lemonade and the 2 cups of Strawberry Syrup in a large pitcher. Taste and add more syrup as needed. Serve over ice garnished with the strawberries.

PECAN OLD FASHIONED

Texas is quickly making its mark in the spirits world, and I plan to sip, shake, and share my excitement for local Texas spirits. I recently had an amazing Old Fashioned cocktail made with Texas bourbon in Austin, and I've been recreating it at home ever since. To create my own twist on this classic cocktail, I add a splash of my Pecan Syrup to the mix.

MAKES 1 COCKTAIL

2 ounces bourbon

¼ ounce Pecan Syrup (page 150)

2 dashes aromatic bitters

Ice

1 piece orange peel, for garnish

3 pecan halves, for garnish

Combine the bourbon, Pecan Syrup, and bitters in a mixing glass and add ice to fill the glass. Stir vigorously with a spoon for 10 seconds.

Strain the mixture into a highball glass filled with ice. Garnish with the orange peel and pecans and serve.

PECAN SODA

Mi mami has graciously given me the honor of hosting Thanksgiving, and I don't take this honor lightly. After all, she was always the ultimate hostess. After figuring out how to serve two turkeys, a few pecan pies, and an endless supply of mashed potatoes for the kids, I thought I had perfected my Thanksgiving menu—that is, until I decided to top my Pecan Syrup with sparkling water. Pecan Soda? Amazing! The kids and adults all agreed: it was the perfect accompaniment to our Thanksgiving meal.

MAKES 1 SODA

Ice

3 to 4 tablespoons Pecan Syrup (page 150)

Sparkling water, for topping

Pecan halves, for garnish

Fill a highball glass with ice. Add the Pecan Syrup, top with the sparkling water, and stir. Garnish with the pecans and serve.

RED WINE PEACH SPRITZER

My little sister and I have a fun tradition of watching late-night chick flicks and then heading to a local restaurant to sip on red wine spritzers. Those few hours away from the kids are our chance to unwind and enjoy a little girl time. This refreshing Red Wine Peach Spritzer is the perfect drink for a girls' night out.

MAKES 4 COCKTAILS

Ice

½ cup Peach Syrup (page 151)

¼ cup freshly squeezed lime juice

1 (750-mL) bottle red wine

Sparkling water, for topping

Sliced fresh peaches, for garnish

Fill 4 wine glasses with ice and add 2 tablespoons of the Peach Syrup and 1 tablespoon of the lime juice to each glass. Add 4 ounces wine and top with the sparkling water. Garnish each glass with the peach slices and serve.

HIBISCUS CHAMPAGNE COCKTAIL

The holidays scream for endless bottles of ice-cold champagne, and with my Hibiscus Syrup, you can easily add a bit of festive holiday color to your cocktail tray. It is the easiest, loveliest cocktail you can imagine, and all you need to make it is Champagne.

SERVES 5

5 tablespoons Hibiscus Syrup
   (page 146)
1 (750-mL) bottle Champagne or
   sparkling wine, chilled

Add 1 tablespoon each of Hibiscus Syrup to 5 champagne glasses and top each with the Champagne. Serve.

HIBISCUS AGUA FRESCA

Agua de jamaica was the first *agua fresca* I tried in Mexico as a child. I was drawn to its intense, ruby-red color. After my first sip, I was hooked. Now I make *agua de jamaica* by the gallon. Instead of heating up my entire kitchen, I rely on my slow cooker to do all the heavy lifting.

SERVES 15 TO 20

12 cups water

3 cups dried hibiscus flowers

2 to 3 cups granulated sugar

1 (4-inch) cinnamon stick
   (optional)

Ice, for serving

Combine the water, the hibiscus flowers, and 2 cups of the sugar in a slow cooker and stir until well combined. Cover and cook on low for 4 hours. Taste and add more of the sugar as desired. Set aside to cool completely.

Strain and serve over ice.

HIBISCUS PUNCH COCKTAIL

This is party punch at its best: *agua de jamaica* is spiked with vodka, lime juice, and plenty of fresh mint. I often make this punch for summer BBQ parties, on days when the Texas sun has us reaching for something refreshing.

SERVES 15 TO 20

2 limes, sliced, plus 10 more lime
   slices for garnish
15 fresh mint leaves, plus 10 more
   for garnish
1 tablespoon granulated sugar
1 batch Hibiscus Agua Fresca
   (page 164)
2 cups vodka
Ice

Combine the 2 sliced limes, the 15 mint leaves, and the sugar in a large punch bowl and muddle gently for 10 seconds, releasing the essential oils of the lime slices and mint leaves.

Pour the Hibiscus Agua Fresca and vodka into the bowl and stir until well combined. Add ice. Garnish with the remaining lime slices and remaining mint leaves and serve.

HIBISCUS CINNAMON MEZCAL COOLERS

On a recent trip to Oaxaca, we sampled plenty of local mezcal. Since returning from that trip, I've been experimenting with mezcal more and more, and this mezcal cooler is one of my favorites. Don't skip dusting the ice in cinnamon sugar, as it adds great character to the cocktail.

MAKES 1 COCKTAIL

2 teaspoons granulated sugar

1 teaspoon ground cinnamon

Ice

½ cup Hibiscus Agua Fresca (page 164)

2 ounces mezcal

Sparkling water, for topping

1 (4-inch) cinnamon stick, for garnish

Mix the sugar and cinnamon together on a small plate.

Fill a glass halfway with ice, add the Hibiscus Agua Fresca and mezcal, and top with sparkling water. Before serving, roll 2 ice cubes in the cinnamon sugar and add them to the glass. Garnish with the cinnamon stick and serve.

RUBY RED PALOMA PUNCH

A true south Texas treasure, ruby red grapefruits flourish in the south Texas soil, which gives them their vibrant, ruby-colored flesh. They are the star of one of my favorite cocktails, the paloma, but as much as I love them, I don't enjoy making them for a crowd in single servings. So I let my slow cooker take the lead, and have it make the most delicious base for my Paloma Punch with plenty of ruby red grapefruit segments.

SERVES 15 TO 20

10 ruby red grapefruits, supremed (segmented)
1 cup freshly squeezed orange juice
1 cup granulated sugar
6 cups tequila blanco
¼ cup freshly squeezed lime juice
1 lime, sliced
Freshly grated zest of 1 lime
4 to 5 cups grapefruit soda (I recommend Fresca, Squirt, or Jarritos brands), for topping
Ice

Place all but 10 of the grapefruit segments in a slow cooker and add the orange juice and sugar. Cover and cook on low for 4 hours. Set aside to cool completely.

Strain the liquid into a punch bowl, pushing on the contents of the strainer with the back of a spoon to ensure that all the liquid is released. Add the tequila, lime juice, lime slices, and lime zest and stir until well combined.

When ready to serve, top with the soda and add the ice and reserved grapefruit segments. Place the bowl at the center of your table and allow your guests to serve themselves.

TEXAS TEA

Mi mami used to make sun tea every day during the summer. She would use a huge glass jug to make a big batch that would last the whole day. She passed this very same glass jug down to me recently. I certainly don't want to run the risk of breaking this precious heirloom, so instead I make my sweet tea in my slow cooker. Of course, I save Mami's jug for our most special occasions.

SERVES 10 TO 12

12 cups water

2 to 3 cups granulated sugar

12 tea bags

Ice

Lemon wedges, for garnish

Combine the water and 2 cups of the sugar in a slow cooker and whisk until thoroughly combined. Add the tea bags, cover, and cook on low for 4 hours.

Strain out and discard the tea bags. Taste and add more of the sugar, if desired.

Pour into a pitcher filled with ice and serve garnished with the lemon wedges.

TEXAS TEA COCKTAIL

Looking for a fun twist on the traditional Texas sweet tea? Try this Texas Tea Cocktail, with a punch of flavor and a splash of vodka.

MAKES 1 COCKTAIL

Ice

½ cup Texas Tea (above)

1½ ounces vodka

1 ounce orange liqueur

Lime slices and 1 (4-inch) cinnamon stick, for garnish

Fill a cocktail shaker with ice. Add the Texas Tea, vodka, and orange liqueur and shake until well chilled.

Strain the mixture into a glass filled with ice. Garnish with the lime slices and a cinnamon stick and serve.

HORCHATA

Traditionally, *horchata* is made by pouring boiling water over rice and almonds, straining through a cloth, and allowing the mixture to sit overnight. These days, it's much easier to use a slow cooker. You simply throw in all of your ingredients, walk away, and let the slow cooker do the work. I give my *horchata* extra richness by adding cinnamon sticks to the mixture. Once they've softened, they're easily blended into the drink, lending it a beautiful cinnamon color.

SERVES 15 TO 20

12 cups water, plus more for blending

3 cups uncooked long-grain white rice

1½ cups granulated sugar, plus more to taste

1 cup raw almonds

3 (4-inch) cinnamon sticks

Ice

Combine 12 cups of water, the rice, 1½ cups of sugar, almonds, and cinnamon sticks in a slow cooker, cover, and cook on low for 2½ hours. Remove the cinnamon sticks.

Working in batches, transfer the contents of the slow cooker to a blender. Cover and blend on high speed until the mixture is nearly smooth (the mixture will still have small bits of rice); add more water if needed. Strain the mixture, taste, and add more sugar if needed.

Serve over ice.

BIG-BATCH HORCHATA MARGARITAS

I love entertaining and creating specialty cocktails for events, but that doesn't mean I want to spend the entire evening shaking them up, one at a time. My Horchata is the perfect base for a unique, creamy margarita. Served in a beautiful punch bowl or drink dispenser, these Big-Batch Horchata Margaritas are the ultimate summer cocktail.

SERVES 15

1 cup granulated sugar and ¼ cup ground cinnamon, for rimming the glass

1 recipe Horchata (page 175)

4 cups tequila blanco

1 cup coconut liqueur

Ice

Mix the sugar and cinnamon together on a small plate. Moisten the rims of 15 margarita glasses and dip the rims in the cinnamon sugar.

Combine the Horchata, tequila, and coconut liqueur in a large pitcher or punch bowl and stir until well combined. Serve over ice in the cinnamon-sugar rimmed glasses.

SLOW-COOKER BLACKBERRY CORDIAL

Blackberries grow abundantly in *mi mami*'s backyard; she always keeps her freezer stocked with them. My grandmother always loved to sip cordials during the holidays, and after she passed away, I made this gorgeous blackberry cordial in memory of her. A splash of blackberry cordial in a cup is the perfect bedtime nightcap.

SERVES 15

10 cups blackberries, frozen
   and thawed
2 cups granulated sugar
12 cups water
2 (4-inch) cinnamon sticks
Freshly grated zest of 1 lemon
½ cup honey
1¼ cups brandy

 Crush together the berries and sugar with a potato masher in a large bowl. Transfer the mixture to a slow cooker and stir in the water, add the cinnamon sticks and lemon zest. Cover and cook on low for 2½ hours.

Stir the mixture, raise the setting to high, and cook for 1½ hours.

Strain the liquid into a punch bowl, pushing on the contents of the strainer with the back of a spoon to ensure that all the liquid is released. Stir in the honey and set aside to cool completely.

Once the mixture has cooled, stir in the brandy and transfer to a sealed container. The mixture will keep in a sealed container in the refrigerator for up to 1 month.

FOUR-BERRY MARGARITAS

Every holiday, I whip up a few batches of homemade margarita mix to give to all of my cocktail-loving friends. I used to let it simmer away on the stove, but now, I use my slow cooker. I set it on low and spend my extra time holiday shopping. Now, you can save time too and give the gift of homemade margarita mix!

SERVINGS VARY

For the Four-Berry Margarita Mix:

12 cups water

1 (32-ounce) bag frozen berry medley

3 cups granulated sugar

2 (4-inch) cinnamon sticks

2 cups freshly squeezed lime juice

To make 1 margarita:

Salt and lime wedge, for rimming

Ice

¼ cup Four-Berry Margarita Mix

1 ounce tequila blanco

1 ounce Cointreau

To make a pitcher of margaritas (serves 4):

Salt and lime wedges, for rimming

1 cup Four-Berry Margarita Mix

1 cup tequila blanco

¼ cup Cointreau

Make the Four-Berry Margarita Mix:

Combine the water, berries, sugar, and cinnamon sticks in a slow cooker. Cover and cook on low for 4 to 6 hours, or until the berries break down. Set aside to cool completely.

Strain the liquid into a large bowl, pushing on the contents of the strainer with the back of a spoon to ensure that all the liquid is released. Stir in the lime juice and evenly divide into four glass bottles, if giving as gifts, or a single large bottle. Chill until ready to use; the mix will keep for up to 2 weeks stored in the refrigerator.

Make 1 Four-Berry Margarita:

Pour the salt on a small plate. Moisten the rim of a margarita glass with the lime wedge and dip the rim in the salt. Fill the margarita glass with ice.

Fill a cocktail shaker with ice and add the Four-Berry Margarita Mix, tequila, and Cointreau. Shake well and strain into the prepared margarita glass. Serve.

Make a pitcher of Four-Berry Margaritas:

Pour the salt on a small plate. Moisten the rims of 4 margarita glasses with the lime wedges and dip the rims in the salt. Fill the margarita glasses with ice.

Combine the Four-Berry Margarita Mix, tequila, and Cointreau in a pitcher and stir until well combined. Divide among the prepared margarita glasses. Serve.

WARM SANGRIA

At our annual *tamalada* (tamale-making party), a nice glass of my Warm Sangria is always a welcome treat. As I prep for the day, I pour everything into my slow cooker and set it on low. By the time my guests arrive, the sangria is ready to serve.

SERVES 8 TO 10

2 (750-mL) bottles red wine

1 pound guavas, seeds removed
   and diced

2 cups tequila reposado

1 cup freshly squeezed orange
   juice

1 apple, cored and diced

1 orange, sliced

1 pear, cored and diced

1 lime, sliced

2 (4-inch) cinnamon sticks

Combine all of the ingredients in a slow cooker, cover, and cook on low for 2 hours.

Serve warm, with each portion getting a share of the fruit.

AGUA DE TAMARINDO

Tamarind (*tamarindo*), a delicious, tart, and sticky-sweet pulp that comes from tree pods, is often used in sauces, marinades, syrups, jams, and candies. But Agua de Tamarindo is the recipe where tamarind really shines. This sweet *agua* is the perfect accompaniment to a plate of tacos, sizzling fajitas, or spicy nachos piled high.

SERVES 10 TO 12

16 tamarind pods

10 cups water

1 cup granulated sugar, plus
   more to taste

Ice

Clean the tamarind pods by removing and discarding the hard outer shells, the stems, and as many strings as you can.

Combine the cleaned tamarind pods, the water, and 1 cup of the sugar in a slow cooker and stir until well combined. Cover and cook on low for 4 hours. Stir and taste for sweetness; add more sugar if needed. Set aside to cool to room temperature.

Strain and serve chilled over the ice.

SPARKLING TAMARIND TEQUILA PUNCH

I can't think of a better way to celebrate than with my sparkling tamarind tequila punch. It's refreshing, easy to make, and always a hit at any gathering. *Salud!*

SERVES 15 TO 20

1 recipe Agua de Tamarindo
  (page 183)
4 cups tequila reposado (see
  note)
1 (16-ounce) bottle sparkling
  water
1 cup freshly squeezed lime juice
Lime slices, for garnish

Fill a large punch bowl with ice. Add the Agua de Tamarindo, tequila, sparkling water, and lime juice and stir until well combined.

Serve the punch in glasses garnished with the lime slices.

NOTE: YOU MAY OMIT THE TEQUILA TO CREATE A FUN MOCKTAIL VERSION OF THIS PARTY PUNCH.

SPIKED CAFÉ DE OLLA

Every few weeks, I like to invite the entire *familia* over for brunch; I make a large batch of Chilaquiles Casserole (page 72), spicy fried potatoes, and plenty of bacon. I also whip up a batch of this yummy, spiked Café de Olla. I prepare the *café* and set out a bottle of tequila reposado and a pitcher of heavy cream so each guest can create (and spike) his or her own.

SERVES 12

12 cups brewed coffee

2 *piloncillo* cones (see page 36)

4 (4-inch) cinnamon sticks

3 to 5 whole star anise (optional)

1 ounce tequila reposado per
   serving (see note)

Heavy cream

Combine the coffee, *piloncillo*, cinnamon sticks, and star anise in a slow cooker. Cover and cook on low for 4 hours, or until all of the *piloncillo* has dissolved.

Stir and reduce the setting to warm. To serve, add 1 ounce of tequila to each mug. Add the *café* to each serving, top with the heavy cream, and serve.

NOTE: THE TEQUILA CAN BE OMITTED TO MAKE A NONALCOHOLIC VERSION OF THIS DELICIOUS DRINK.

HOT COCOA FOUR WAYS

The week before Christmas is a magical time for our family. Every year, we plan a week of activities for the kids. We have movie nights, we make ornaments, we play Christmas bingo, we bake holiday cookies, we go for caroling hayrides, and my youngest daughter hosts a Christmas cocoa party at our home. She makes four cocoas, decorates the table with plenty of Christmas treats, and leads us through a holiday DIY craft. I've recreated her creations for the slow cooker. We may not get snow in Texas, but we have plenty of fun spreading holiday cheer!

MEXICAN CHOCOLATE HOT COCOA

Our Mexican chocolate cocoa is creamy, rich, and the perfect treat after holiday caroling with the kids. *Piloncillo* adds a touch of warmth to this classic Mexican hot cocoa drink.

SERVES 6 TO 8

½ gallon whole milk

2 cups chocolate chips, plus more for serving

⅓ cup unsweetened cocoa powder

¼ cup freshly grated *piloncillo* (see page 36) or light brown sugar

1 tablespoon vanilla extract

¼ teaspoon salt

2 (4-inch) cinnamon sticks, plus more for serving

Combine the milk, 2 cups of the chocolate chips, the cocoa powder, *piloncillo*, vanilla extract, salt, and 2 cinnamon sticks in a slow cooker. Cover and cook on low, whisking occasionally, for 2 hours.

Set the slow cooker to warm and whisk thoroughly before serving. Serve warm garnished with more of the chocolate chips and cinnamon sticks.

DULCE DE LECHE HOT COCOA

Dulce de leche makes everything better, so of course I had to create a spin on traditional hot cocoa that included one of my favorite sweet ingredients. You'll love the addition of dulce de leche, because it creates a thicker, richer, and creamier hot cocoa your whole family will love.

SERVES 6 TO 8

½ gallon whole milk

2 cups heavy whipping cream

1 (14-ounce) can sweetened condensed milk

1 cup dulce de leche

1 cup white chocolate chips

1 teaspoon vanilla extract

Combine the milk, cream, condensed milk, dulce de leche, chocolate chips, and vanilla in a slow cooker. Cover and cook on low, whisking occasionally, for 2 hours.

Set the slow cooker to warm and whisk thoroughly before serving. Serve warm.

MAZAPAN HOT COCOA

Mi cariño (my husband) is addicted to mazapan, a Mexican candy made from ground peanuts. When he was deployed in Iraq, *mi papi* (my dad) would send him cases of mazapanes to enjoy and share with his fellow soldiers. When the holidays roll around this recipe is his only request—mazapan hot cocoa.

SERVES 6 TO 8

½ gallon whole milk

2 cups heavy whipping cream

1 (14-ounce) can sweetened condensed milk

5 (1-ounce) mazapan candy bars, broken into small pieces

1 teaspoon vanilla extract

Combine the milk, cream, condensed milk, mazapan bars, and vanilla in a slow cooker. Cover and cook on low, whisking occasionally, for 2 hours.

Set the slow cooker to warm and whisk thoroughly before serving. Serve warm.

CHOCOLATE-PECAN PIE HOT COCOA

Texans make the best pecan pie, so it's only natural that it would eventually become a holiday treat here. This cocoa is super rich, creamy, and, of course, packed with chocolate and pecan flavor.

SERVES 6 TO 8

½ gallon whole milk

2 cups heavy whipping cream

2 cups chocolate chips

1 (14-ounce) can sweetened condensed milk

½ cup Pecan Syrup (page 150), plus more to taste

Pecan halves, for garnish

Combine the milk, cream, chocolate chips, condensed milk, and Pecan Syrup in a slow cooker. Cover and cook on low, whisking occasionally, for 2 hours.

Set the slow cooker to warm and whisk thoroughly before serving; taste and add more Pecan Syrup, if desired. Serve warm garnished with the pecans.

GUAVA CHAMPAGNE PUNCH

Guavas remind me of my *abuelito*. He had a small guava tree in his backyard and ate them so much, he often smelled of them. I wanted to combine that wonderful memory with something else I love—ice-cold Champagne—so I created this gorgeous Guava Champagne Punch to perfectly pair the two.

SERVES 8 TO 10

6 pounds guavas, sliced in half

2 cups granulated sugar

1½ cups water

¼ cup freshly squeezed lemon juice

Ice

2 (750-mL) bottles chilled Champagne or sparkling wine

Combine the sliced guavas, sugar, water, and lemon juice in a slow cooker. Cover and cook on low for 6 to 8 hours. After 6 hours, check the guavas for doneness, as slow cookers' temperatures can vary. If they have not yet broken down, cook for 30 more minutes.

Using a fine mesh sieve, strain the liquid into a container, pushing on the contents of the strainer with the back of a spoon to ensure that all the liquid is released. Refrigerate immediately for at least 1 hour; the syrup should be chilled when used.

Fill a punch bowl with ice and add the chilled guava syrup and Champagne. Stir lightly until just combined and serve.

NOTE: THE GUAVA SYRUP CAN BE MADE UP TO 3 DAYS IN ADVANCE AND STORED IN THE REFRIGERATOR UNTIL READY TO USE.

ACKNOWLEDGMENTS

Gracias to *mi familia* for the continued support in all that encompasses *Sweet Life*. From our midnight grocery runs to the continuous loading of the dishwasher to all the road trips, this journey wouldn't be half the fun without y'all. Roy, thank you for always being there to lift me, love me, and encourage me to keep on creating. Pips, your endless spark of imagination inspires me to stay young and thank you, thank you, for reminding me that life is simply better with butter. Roy, Angelica, and Lisandra, we are truly living the *Sweet Life*. I love y'all.

To Lava, my big sister Lava, for opening her house to accommodate me in my photo shoots, videos, and fiestas.

To Jason, thank you for joining me on my first solo project and capturing my food with such ease and elegance. I look forward to many more projects with you.

To the entire Countryman and W. W. Norton team, thank you for taking a chance on this *Tejana* and for allowing me to share my love of Tex-Mex food. Big thanks to Aurora for the endless emails and phone calls, and for enjoying my salsa verde.

Here's to the love of slow cookers!

AUTHOR'S NOTE

I grew up in the Coastal Bend town of Aransas Pass, Texas, a place known for its fresh seafood and family dinners where everyone is invited to the table.

When Hurricane Harvey made landfall in our small town, we lost so much, but we never lost our hope, our strength, or our determination. I feel blessed to have grown up in a place where family means community.

In Aransas Pass after Hurricane Harvey, there was no lack of compassion or kindness. Families, businesses, and first responders all pitched together to cut away branches, clean properties, and prepare meals for our hungry neighbors. Our pantries and fridges might have been empty, but our bellies and hearts were full.

The recipes in this cookbook are dedicated to my community, *mi familia*, in Aransas Pass. Their resilience and endurance makes me even prouder to be an Aransas girl. #SoyTejana #AransasStrong

INDEX

For information about permission to reproduce selections from
this book, write to Permissions, The Countryman Press,
500 Fifth Avenue, New York, NY 10110

For information about special discounts for bulk purchases,
please contact W. W. Norton Special Sales at
specialsales@wwnorton.com or 800-233-4830

Manufacturing through Regent Publishing Services
Book design by Anna Reich
Production manager: Devon Zahn

The Countryman Press
www.countrymanpress.com

A division of W. W. Norton & Company, Inc.
500 Fifth Avenue, New York, NY 10110
www.wwnorton.com

978-1-168268-126-8

10 9 8 7 6 5 4 3 2 1